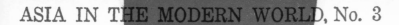

472
6

CHINA AT THE WASHINGTON CONFERENCE 1921·1922

by WUNSZ KING

ASIA IN THE MODERN WORLD, NO. 3

CHINA AT THE WASHINGTON CONFERENCE 1921·1922

by WUNSZ KING

St. John's University Press, New York
1963

Published by the University Press under the auspices
of the Institute of Asian Studies and Copyright 1963 ©
by St. John's University

Library of Congress Catalog Card Number 63-14976

FOREWORD

The author of this monograph is an experienced writer on questions relating to China's foreign relations. He has published, in Chinese and English, a number of pamphlets and articles in the same field. His most recent contribution concerning China's part in the Paris Peace Conference—especially the Shantung question—was well received by those who are interested in China and the Far East.

Mr. Wunsz King's present treatise on China at the Washington Conference is a natural sequel to his earlier pamphlet. This Conference, certainly insofar as its Far Eastern Commission and the special arrangement for the Sino-Japanese negotiations with a view to the settlement of the Shantung question were concerned, had its origin in the failure of the Paris Peace Conference to do justice to China. Her important claims, presented as much for the general cause of world peace as in the particular interest of China's well-being as a nation, were not given the consideration and satisfaction they merited. It remained for the far-seeing statesmen of Washington to initiate a collective international effort to redress the wrongs perpetrated at the Paris Conference.

I have known Mr. King for over forty years. He joined my legation in Washington in 1919 and thereafter became one of my closest colleagues in many an international conference which I attended as China's chief delegate. He has always been a conscientious student of international problems. With scholarly training and an investigative mind, he spared no effort to be accurate in his conclusions. In the preparation of the present monograph, I understand that he has not only used first-hand materials he had collected while attending the Washington Conference, but has also consulted original documents from Chinese and United States official sources.

I recall, with appreciation, how Mr. King helped me at the Washington Conference in connection with the customs tariff problem. In fact, as early as the autumn of 1918 when, with the approval of the Chinese Minister of Foreign Affairs in Peking, I set up a special committee to prepare for China's participation in the Paris Peace Conference, I asked Mr. King to work on this question with a view to recovering China's tariff autonomy. Since that time he has justly been recognized as an authority in this field. On several occasions, he served as China's chief delegate to the international conferences on trade and tariff matters, including the Havana Conference in 1948.

Besides his talent for research and his habit of industry, Mr. King has the added advantage of being able to marshal facts with an excellent control for accuracy. He also writes English with lucidity and precision.

The Institute of Asian Studies of St. John's University is to be congratulated for sponsoring Mr. King's interesting and valuable work.

V. K. Wellington Koo

The Hague
Dec. 1, 1962

PREFACE

The 1921-1922 Washington Conference was particularly significant for China and the entire East Asian world. No serious student or observer of our China policy can afford to neglect this first-hand account of the Conference.

Mr. Wunsz King, until recently Chinese Ambassador to Belgium, was a member of the Chinese Delegation to this Conference, which discussed in extensive detail the Shantung problem and other serious problems of the Far East. Mr. King here presents his personal impressions of the Conference. As many significant developments at this Conference have never been published in any Western language, this monograph is of some importance to the increasing number of students concerned with the modern history of China.

As coordinator of this series, I feel most grateful to the author for his cooperation in making this study available and also to Dr. V. K. Wellington Koo for writing the Foreword. Dr. Koo, as a delegate of China, played a leading role at this Conference.

Paul K. T. Sih, *Director*
Institute of Asian Studies
St. John's University

CHINA AT THE WASHINGTON CONFERENCE, 1921-22

The end of the Great War of 1914-18 found the world atmosphere conducive to setting up a new international order. The Central European Powers were defeated; ambitious Japan needed time to consolidate the spoils of victory; Bolshevist Russia was still too weak to count in international affairs; and the victorious allies apparently desired peace and were capable of enforcing it. For a war-weary world it seemed that no moment in recent history was more propitious for establishing international peace on firm and lasting foundations.

There was, however, a darker side to the picture: the League of Nations had come into existence without United States membership. The Versailles treaty, the Covenant of the League, and the Shantung settlement had aroused strong opposition to Woodrow Wilson both inside and outside the American Congress. Although he did his best to salvage the monumental achievements of the Paris Conference, Wilson failed to win the support of the American isolationists and conservative elements. The reluctance of the United States to join the League had grave consequences for the political stability of the Far East.

The center of potential threats to peace had swung like a pendulum, from West to East. The causes of discord and friction in the Pacific islands and the Far East had to be forestalled and eventually removed. Relations between China and Japan needed immediate improvement; relations between China and the other allied powers needed clarification. Political tensions and economic necessity demanded the immediate reduction of the naval armaments of the great powers. With this object in view the next American presi-

1

dent, Warren G. Harding, took the initiative in calling the Washington Conference.[1]

Two different groups of questions needed examination: first, the limitation of armaments; second, the situation in the Pacific and Far East. The countries concerned with the first group of questions comprised the five principal allied and associated powers, namely the United States, Great Britain, France, Italy, and Japan. Nine powers took part in the discussions on the second group of questions: the five powers just mentioned plus China, Belgium, the Netherlands, and Portugal. This classification of the participants into two groups—those with general interest and others of limited interest in world affairs—was undoubtedly a legacy from the Paris Conference.

In the composition of the American delegation to the Conference, the new Republican president wisely sought to ensure bipartisan support for the new agreements by asking representatives of both the majority and the minority parties to serve. Harding had learned a painful but useful lesson when his predecessor's commitments in Paris were repudiated by Congress. Harding was completely aware that the Senate was extremely jealous of its Constitutional right to give advice and consent to foreign policy. Since then the United States has usually followed his precedent in sending two-party delegations to international conferences.

China appointed four delegates to the Conference, namely: Sao-ke Alfred Sze, Minister in Washington; V. K. Wellington Koo, Minister in London; Chung-hui Wang, Chief Justice of the Supreme Court of China; and Chao-chu Wu. Wu was to represent South China. His father, Wu Ting-fang, at one time an envoy in Washington near the end of the Manchu dynasty, was then Foreign Minister in the Canton government under the presidency of Sun Yat-sen. Chao-chu Wu, the son, who served as his father's vice-minister, did not even go to Washington. The Chinese delegation, some 140 persons in all, included two Superior Advisers: Yuho M. T. Liang, former Minister for Foreign

Affairs; and Tzu-chi Chow, former Minister of Finance. These two elder statesmen delivered a special message to the three attending delegates from the President of the Republic, Hsu Shih-chang, expressing his confidence that they would cooperate harmoniously among themselves in assuming the heavy responsibilities of the delegation.

The Conference opened in Continental Hall on November 12, 1921. President Harding delivered the welcome address. Charles Evans Hughes, the United States Secretary of State, was elected chairman. With his firm voice and bearded countenance, he was an excellent choice as a symbol of authority in the chair. The Conference then proceeded to form two Committees of the Whole to consider the two lists of questions simultaneously though separately, since they were interrelated in character and required an interdependent settlement. The first Committee of the Whole was the Committee on the Limitation of Armament. The other was the Committee on the Pacific and Far Eastern Questions. All three Chinese delegates from the Central Government attended this latter committee. Each of them acted as the spokesman for the delegation when he had a proposition to submit or a viewpoint to defend in connection with the matter specifically assigned him for handling. With the exception of items relating to some Pacific islands and Eastern Siberia, the entire program on the Pacific and Far Eastern questions was devoted almost exclusively to the examination of Chinese problems. Indeed, it looked as though the formidable collection of unequal treaties and other related matters had been brought to Washington for thorough review or abrogation. This long list ranged from such relatively simple topics as the abolition of foreign postal agencies and radio stations to the far more complex problems of restoring tariff autonomy and relinquishing extraterritorial rights. There was also, of course, the all-important question of Shantung. The three Chinese delegates had distributed all these subjects among themselves for study and negotiation. In addition to his many other duties, for example, Sze, the

3

chief delegate, presented China's program of ten points.[2] Similarly, Wang, a prominent jurist, negotiated the question of extraterritoriality and did much drafting work; and Koo, an experienced diplomatist, took charge of questions relating to the customs tariff and those relating to leased territories. Koo also sat on four of seven sub-committees. As is customary in international conferences, the Committee of the Whole, after general discussion of a particular topic, referred it to a sub-committee for more thorough study. Conclusions reached in the sub-committee were then sent back to the full committee for decision. The decisions of the committee were then reported to the plenary session of the Conference for adoption.

A number of these decisions took the form of simple resolutions which were adopted by the Conference at its various plenary sessions. Except as specified below, they were adopted in the name of the nine powers. These resolutions concerned the following items:

(1) Establishment of a Board of Reference for Far Eastern questions;

(2) Relinquishment of extraterritoriality (with China concurring in virtue of an additional resolution);

(3) Abolition of foreign postal agencies (agreed to by the four powers having such post offices in China, namely, Japan, France, Great Britain, and the United States);

(4) Withdrawal of foreign armed forces (China not voting);

(5) Elimination of foreign radio stations;

(6) Unification of Chinese railways;

(7) Reduction of Chinese armed forces;

(8) Review of commitments of China or with respect to China;

(9) Possession and control of the Chinese Eastern Rail-

way (China taking no part in one of the two resolutions).

With the exception of the postal agencies and radio stations, however, these resolutions by themselves offered no definite solutions to the problems involved. At best they either provided a procedure or machinery for taking action in the distant though not exactly undefined future, or else they simply expressed a hope or a wish to that end. The deliberations leading to this series of resolutions were, nevertheless, quite useful. They served to clarify and officially record the opposing views.

Altogether there were seven plenary or public sessions. The last one, held on February 6, 1922, witnessed the decorous ceremony of the signing of four treaties. Harding gave the closing speech and bade farewell to the distinguished guests. The Conference adjourned *sine die* and the guests departed in high spirits. The Five Power Treaty limiting naval armament aimed at abolishing naval competition by fixing, among other things, a maximum tonnage of capital ships at the ratios of 5:5:3 for Great Britain, the United States, and Japan respectively. At the same time, these Powers pledged themselves not to establish new fortifications or naval bases on the Pacific islands. In addition there were two Nine Power Treaties: one defined the principles and policies to be followed in matters concerning China; the other made some new provisions for the Chinese customs tariff. Through a unique diplomatic procedure described below, the representatives of China and Japan had conducted the Shantung conversations during and yet outside the Conference. They signed a special agreement on February 4 which was simply reported to the Conference.

The Conference, having thus been in session for two and a half months from November 1921 to February 1922, was adjourned in the same noble spirit and in the same friendly atmosphere in which it had been convened. In President Harding's words:[3]

It has been the fortune of this Conference to sit in a day far enough removed from war's bitterness, yet near enough to war's horrors, to gain the benefit of both the hatred of war and the yearning for peace . . . The world demands a sober contemplation of the existing order and the realization that there can be no cure without sacrifice, not by one of us, but by all of us . . . I do not mean surrendered rights, or narrowed freedom, or denied aspirations, or ignored national necessities. . . . No pride need be humbled, no nationality submerged, but I would have a [merging] of minds committing all of us to less preparation for war and more enjoyment of fortunate peace. . . . When the days were dragging and agreements were delayed, when there were obstacles within and hindrances without, few stopped to realize that here was a conference of sovereign Powers where only unanimous agreement could be made the rule. Majorities could not decide without impinging [on] national rights. There were no victors to command, no vanquished to yield. All had voluntarily to agree in translating the conscience of our civilization and give concrete expression to world opinion. . . . And you have agreed in spite of all difficulties, and the agreements are proclaimed to the world.

And then in a vein of optimism for the future, Harding had this to say:

It little matters what we appraise as the outstanding accomplishments. Any one of them alone would have justified the Conference. But the whole achievement has so cleared the atmosphere that it will seem like breathing the refreshing air of a new morn of promise.

It is proposed in the following pages to focus attention on the three topics of Shantung and the two Nine Power Treaties. A few other matters of related historical interest will also be taken up in a more concise manner.

Shantung[4]

At Paris the Chinese delegation could not have expected the political foes of President Wilson to weave the Shantung issue into the fabric of party politics. Shantung and Kiaochow soon were prominent in the American press, in public speeches, in Senate debate, and above all in the list of proposed amendments and reservations to the German Peace Treaty. The opposition was loud and abusive. The recalcitrant legislators raised strong objections to several issues besides Shantung. Yet the average man could more readily understand the injustice of surrendering a piece of Chinese territory to Japan than could he understand, for instance, the intricacies and implications of Article 10 of the Covenant. Thus, Shantung played an important part in determining the fate of that great historical document.

The interval between the two conferences saw the deployment of a variety of diplomatic maneuvers in connection with Shantung. Washington, and to a lesser degree London, exerted pressure on Japan to honor her promise to restore Kiaochow and other rights to China. These efforts, however, were again fruitless. The only result was an unsatisfactory declaration made by the Japanese Foreign Minister, Yasuya Uchida, on August 2, 1919,[5] which only confirmed the decision of the Council of Three. In plainer language, the Japanese suggested that a policeman having recovered a stolen purse is entitled to keep its contents while returning the empty purse to the owner. The series of notes subsequently exchanged between China and Japan did not bring about any progress. Both sides were firmly entrenched in their respective positions. Japan repeatedly proposed opening direct negotiations on her terms. China flatly declined to negotiate on such terms. Then in December 1920, the inaugural Assembly of the League of Nations convened in Geneva. China had at one time contemplated presenting the Shantung case to the League. Eventually she refrained from doing so, realizing that the move would be meaningless without United States membership. It was also feared that this might diminish China's chance of obtaining the non-permanent seat in the Council she was seeking. China, even later, did not take this step, although, thanks to

Koo's careful planning, she was subsequently elected to the Council. On the eve of the Washington Conference, Hughes, informally approached by Japan, attempted to bring the two parties together, though without much enthusiasm on either side.[6] At any rate the indirect effort made by the United States met with no more success than the repeated efforts made by Japan directly. The stalemate remained unbroken pending the convening of the conference.

Mindful of public opinion on the home front, China resisted all overtures for direct negotiations with her Eastern neighbor. Instead, she manifested a readiness to accept the good offices of a third power or an international conference. The impending Conference furnished precisely the opportunity she had been seeking. The United States, however, dissuaded her from bringing up the Shantung question because most of the participating countries would object to it, on the ground that they were themselves bound by the Shantung clauses in the Versailles treaty. Japan, on the other hand, opposed and resented all such attempts at solution. Probably she was haunted by unpleasant memories of the intervention by Russia, France, and Germany in connection with the China-Japan treaty of Shimonoseki (1895). Japan doubtless had the Shantung question in mind when, on July 26, 1921, she conditionally accepted the invitation to the conference: Such matters "as are of sole concern to certain particular Powers or such matters that may be regarded accomplished facts should be scrupulously avoided."[7] In other words, Japan wished to exclude the Shantung problem from the agenda. In Harding's formal invitation on August 11 we find this carefully worded formula:

It is not the purpose of this Government to attempt to define the scope of the discussion in relation to the Pacific and Far East, but rather to leave this to be the subject of suggestions to be exchanged before the meeting of the Conference in the expectation that the spirit of friendship and

8

a cordial appreciation of the importance of the elimination of sources of controversy will govern the final decision.[8]

It was due to the efforts of the chief delegates of the two principal powers, namely, Hughes of the United States and Arthur J. Balfour of the British Empire, that the Sino-Japanese conversations on Shantung became a reality and eventually a success. As indicated above, the conversations were held between the Chinese and Japanese representatives during the Conference and yet technically detached from it. While these conversations were designed to solve the most urgent problem affecting good relationships in the Far East, and while they actually took place in the very building in which the committees and sub-committees of the Conference had their meetings, these conversations nevertheless did not find their way into the agenda. Curious as this seems, it must be remembered that what was really important was the presence of the neutral observers at the conversations. For the proud Chinese, to carry on informal conversations with the Japanese was less objectionable than to negotiate with them. The presence of observers rendered the conversations somewhat less direct in appearance, created an agreeable atmosphere, and helped to strengthen the morale of the Chinese representatives. Since the conversations were not held in Peking or Tokyo but in Washington a neutral setting was assured. Furthermore, in informal discussions both sides could refrain from relying on potentially embarrassing treaty commitments.[9] For the equally proud Japanese the bilateral character of the conversation was most important. They hoped that the observers would remain silent spectators. The Japanese soon found an occasion to have their own real intentions in this matter revealed. Despite their divergent views, however, both sides perceived the wisdom of swallowing a bit of their *amour propre* and of giving mutual concessions on procedure. In this spirit the contending parties, at long last, agreed to sit down at the same table.

As had been prearranged behind the scene, the honor fell on the chief Japanese delegate, Baron T. Kato, to make, during the tenth meeting of the Committee of the Whole, held on November 30, 1921,[10] an official announcement about the opening of the conversations. The chief Chinese delegate, Sze, accepted the good offices proposal. But he pointed out that the Chinese delegation had not solicited it and that they reserved their freedom to seek other methods of settlement in case of their inability to agree on a fair and just solution. On the following day, the first meeting was held in the Pan American Union building. The three Chinese delegates attended this and all subsequent meetings. Kato, Prince Tokugawa and Hanihara represented Japan. The first two men were subsequently replaced by Debuchi and Baron Shidehara. Kijuro Shidehara, then Ambassador in Washington, was noted for his inclination to show some conciliation and friendliness towards China in Japan's dealings with her. It might be said of him, in present-day parlance, that he had preferred the theory of peaceful coexistence to that of the inevitability of war. It was he, moreover, who, as a leader of the Minseito party and of the young liberals in Japan, for a time exercised a considerable degree of restraining influence vis-à-vis the Japanese extremists. Indeed, Shidehara was the embodiment of the good neighbor policy toward China known as the Shidehara policy. The chapter of the Shantung conversations in the history of the Sino-Japanese diplomatic relations was in fact characterized by a battle of wits between this Japanese statesman and Wellington Koo, the principal spokesmen for the two delegations.

The opening meeting was also honored by the presence of the leaders of the American and British delegations, Hughes and Balfour, who had convened the meeting. Both men indicated their readiness to render services should circumstances call for their friendly intervention. They then withdrew and left the conduct of the conversations entirely in the hands of the Chinese and Japanese representatives in the presence of the observers. Among these may be mentioned John V. A. MacMurray for the United States and Miles W. Lampson for Great Britain. The former was at that time Chief of the Far Eastern Division of the State Department; the latter was a member of the British Foreign Office. Both diplomats in later years served as Ministers to China.

The two delegations then agreed upon the following procedure: The meetings should be informal; there would be no chairman or agenda; as much publicity as possible would be given to the proceedings; at the close of each meeting the date would be fixed for the next meeting. Altogether there were thirty-six meetings in the course of two months from December 1, 1921, to January 31, 1922, with a New Year recess for fortnight and then a longer adjournment over the railway question. There were altogether eleven items for discussion and settlement. Mere enumeration will show sufficiently the immensity of the tasks and complexity of the problems involved. These items were, in the order of their arrangement in the final treaty, as follows:

 (1) Restoration of Kiaochow;

 (2) Transfer of public properties;

 (3) Withdrawal of Japanese troops;

 (4) Maritime Customs at Tsingtao;

 (5) Tsingtao-Tsinanfu Railway;

 (6) Extensions of the Tsingtao-Tsinanfu Railway;

 (7) Mines;

 (8) Opening of Kiaochow;

 (9) Salt industry;

(10) Submarine cables;

(11) Wireless stations.

To be sure, there were in addition to the railway question many other issues—the public properties and the salt industry questions for instance—which gave rise to certain difficulties. But those difficulties were, relatively speaking, easily overcome. The railway question was the most difficult of all. Nearly one half of the meetings were devoted to the consideration of that single item. In truth, the railway question proved to be the core of the entire Shantung controversy. Only a statesmanlike effort to solve it would bring about fruitful negotiations.

At the turn of the century, Germany, having acquired this particular railway concession from the Chinese government, granted a special charter to a corporation known as the *Schantung Eisenbahn-Gesellschaft* to construct and operate the Tsingtao-Tsinanfu railway, also called the Kiaochow-Tsinan railway. Some 290 miles long, the line runs from the fine, deep-water harbor of Tsingtao westward to the strategic city of Tsinan, capital of Shantung province. At Tsinan it connects with the British-German financed Tientsin-Pukow railway, a trunk line some 600 miles long running from Tientsin southward to Pukow and thence to Nanking. The Tsingtao-Tsinanfu line traverses the heart of the Shantung Peninsula—a land rich in agricultural produce and mineral resources. At the close of the last century, control or possession by a foreign power of a railroad or a network of railroads in the territory of China carried with it all the evils of imperialism: economic exploitation, political penetration, and even military threats. Inevitably, this led to the demarcation of a sphere of interest or influence in favour of that power and at the expense of China. The Russian-controlled Chinese Eastern railway and the Japanese-controlled South Manchurian railway were only the most notorious and most flagrant examples of this abuse. If there were any difference regarding the Tsingtao-Tsinan railway, it was only one of degree rather than kind.

With this historical background in mind, it is easy to understand why the Chinese delegation had to exercise great circumspection. On December 2, at the second meeting, a general discussion of the railway question took place. The Japanese reiterated the original proposal of operating the line as a joint Sino-Japanese enterprise. This, it will be recalled, not only represented the considered policy of the Japanese government but was also—question of validity quite apart—the subject matter of an exchange of notes between the two countries, and therefore a commitment on the part of China. This proposal provoked a sharp rejoinder from Koo: "It was something like the matrimonial contract which would not be a success if the contracting parties were forced into it."[11] At Hanihara's request, it was decided that the railway question should be postponed and that easier questions should be taken up first at the next meetings. So far as Japan was concerned, a joint enterprise would redound to her best interests. She could then contrive to monopolize and to perpetuate her control of the railway. As a tentative substitute, pending the approval of Tokyo, the Japanese delegation brought forward a plan whereby China was to seek a long-term loan from Japanese bankers for the purchase of the railway and, during the currency of the loan, to engage a chief engineer, a traffic manager, and a chief accountant—all to be of Japanese nationality and recommended by the Japanese financiers. The question of the monetary value of the railway[12] was agreed to without difficulty: it was to be the amount which had been assessed by the Reparations Commission at Paris for deduction from the total of the pecuniary reparations due from Germany to Japan, plus the cost of certain additions and improvements, minus depreciation. The term "Reparations Commission figure" was not used because of Chinese opposition. As was to be expected, the plan of a Japanese loan encountered serious objections from the Chinese. Instead, they offered to make a single cash payment with Chinese money, an offer which sounded more patriotic than practicable; and later offered to spread the payment over six installments extending over three years. In turn, these counter-proposals were unacceptable to the Japanese. Shidehara insisted on a Japanese loan to be coupled with the employment of Japanese officials in a manner similar to other railway contracts by which non-Chinese officials had been employed. In plain terms he ascribed the gradual growth of this practice to the alleged inefficiency, mismanagement, and corruption on the part of the Chinese railway administration. Koo, while characterizing the accusations thus made as being "rather severe strictures" which the Chinese "hardly deserved," sought to bring the point in clear perspective by observing that—

The practice of employing foreign experts had grown up not from any dissatisfaction on the part of foreign financiers, but from the fact that in building railways China had had to borrow foreign capital and that, in making railway loan contracts, foreign bankers had used the opportunity to ask for these various offices. But in the case of the Shantung railway loan, the road was already in operation. It evidently stood in a different class from the railways which were merely projected and for which the necessary fund for construction had to be financed.[13]

When his Japanese counterpart explained that those officers would not control the railway, Koo had no hesitation in challenging him to deny that the "power to recommend candidates for those important posts to the Chinese government, with the implication that they should be accepted, would constitute an important element of control."[14]

The New Year recess was to enable the Japanese delegates to consult with their government. By then the railway dispute had practically been narrowed to the question of acceptance or rejection of the Japanese proposal for the participation of Japanese technical men in the service of the railway administration. The Japanese gave the impression that if this demand could be satisfied, they would also subscribe to the idea of payment by means of Chinese government treasury notes. The Chinese as a conciliatory gesture offered to employ a Japanese engineer but not the other two experts, not even in the capacity of associate or assistant officials. The willingness of the Chinese to meet,

14

as far as possible, the wishes of the Japanese delegation, as Sze put it, did not help much. Since the Japanese did not attach much importance to the post of the engineer, they soon dropped their demand for it, thinking that by so doing they too had shown some sort of compromise.

Such was the situation when it was suddenly further complicated by internal politics in China. In December 1921, Liang Shih-yi, a veteran politician and an able financier, became the new Premier, with Yen Hui-ching (W. W. Yen) as Foreign Minister. Liang's appointment was recommended by Chang Tso-lin, a powerful war lord in the three provinces of Manchuria. But Chang had a deadly foe in the person of another powerful war lord in the central provinces, Wu Pei-fu. As for Yen, his personal sympathy leaned rather towards Wu than towards Chang.

On the 29th of that month, Torikichi Obata, the Japanese Minister in Peking, called on the new Premier. Obata was the Japanese diplomat who, as a counsellor sitting at the negotiations of the Twenty-one Demands, incurred the resentment of the Chinese because of his contemptuous and uncompromising attitude toward China. In later years he was considered *persona non grata* by China when Japan proposed him to be the envoy in Nanking. During that interview with the new Chinese premier, replying to an anxious inquiry made by Obata as to how the Shantung railway issue was to be solved, Liang told him (according to a brief telegram sent by the Waichiaopu, the Chinese Ministry of Foreign Affairs, to the three delegates two days later) that a loan would be sought and the railway operated under Chinese management but that details would be arranged in Washington.[15] While a "loan" here was meant to be in Chinese government treasury notes, as was made clear in a subsequent telegram from the Waichiaopu to the delegates on January 5, 1922,[16] almost coinciding with the first sign of anger on Wu Pei-fu's part, this mysterious word standing alone was nevertheless susceptible of more interpretations than one. And so it definitely was, for it did not

15

rule out an arrangement with Japanese financiers. Moreover, if details were left to be discussed in Washington, it would certainly presuppose the conclusion of an agreement in Peking. Unfortunately, therefore, it was this interview which left behind it a trail of genuine misgivings; added fuel to the smouldering fire of civil war; and worst of all, from the diplomatic point of view, gave the Japanese occasion to read into the talk something which could not and should not have been intended. Thus, on January 4, 1922, Shidehara told Hughes that Premier Liang had made to Obata a proposal which was very similar to the one the Japanese delegation had brought forward in Washington, namely, a railway loan on terms similar to those recently made in connection with other railways in China where foreign nationals were interested.[17] In other words, as the American Secretary of State interpreted it, Liang was "personally disposed to accept an arrangement for the purchase of the railway by means of a Japanese long term loan."[18] It was thus clear that the report of the alleged readiness on the part of the new Premier to accede to Japanese terms had originated from the Japanese delegation.[19] It gave rise to perturbation among the Americans and the Chinese alike. It came as a bolt from the blue especially to the Chinese delegates. One of them, C. H. Wang, is said to have privately expressed his personal doubt whether the delegation could even continue to claim limited representation for Peking.[20]

It was true that Obata had similarly sounded Yen about his views in regard to the Japanese proposal of a railway loan. Two days previously, on December 27, he had called on the Foreign Minister[21] to press for a definite answer as to whether the Chinese government would accept it and threatened to break off conversations in the event of its rejection. Yen was opposed to the proposal, although he did not expressly say so to the caller. They had a lengthy discussion in the course of which the Foreign Minister stressed that the difficulty was caused by Japan's stubborn

16

attitude toward the two questions of financing the line and the employment of experts. In the end, Yen told Obata that the matter would be considered at a cabinet meeting. While this non-committal attitude could lend itself to more than one interpretation, it was presumably motivated by the desire to avoid an immediate rupture in the Washington negotiations. The Yen-Obata interview was unknown to the public. At any rate the war lord in central China had singled out the Prime Minister and not the Foreign Minister as the target for condemnation.

Taking the interview with the Premier as a pretext, Wu Pei-fu lost no time in launching a violent campaign against Liang and in demanding his resignation. Although the angry words and demonstrations were directed against Liang, they were actually meant for the Manchurian war lord, Chang. In one of his strongly worded circular telegrams, basing himself on a rather irresponsible telegram sent to him by the "people's delegates" who were in Washington observing the Conference, Wu Pei-fu charged that "Premier Liang has telegraphed to the Chinese delegates stating that the demands of redeeming [the] Shantung railway with a Japanese loan and the Sino-Japanese management by the Japanese have been accepted by the Central Government."[22] Again, on the side of Canton, Wu Ting-fang, presumably relying on some press reports, made the accusation that Liang had been planning to borrow Japanese money in order to meet the Chinese New Year requirements for the Peking government.[23]

Liang, on his part, also issued a series of declarations in which he not only denied having talked with anybody in favor of a Japanese loan for the redemption of the railway, but also confirmed the stand the Chinese delegation had been taking. He emphasized that the Japanese visitor had paid a mere courtesy call. As regards the railway, he declared publicly that he would personally pledge one-tenth of the total amount for its immediate purchase.[24]

For a while all this turmoil at home imposed silence on

the delegates abroad. It was not until January 10, four days after the complete deadlock of the Sino-Japanese conversations, that the delegates cabled to the Cabinet and the Waichiaopu jointly, reporting the information which had emanated from the Japanese delegation and asking for verification. This inquiry drew forth a most emphatic denial from the Chinese government.[25] Meanwhile, however, the attacks on Liang increased in scope and in violence, so much so that finally he had to offer his resignation, was granted sick leave, and left Peking for Tientsin. Yen acted concurrently as premier during Liang's absence.

Chang Tso-lin made energetic efforts to defend his friend. He demanded proof of Wu's charges against Liang and asserted that if every new premier could be so attacked and driven out of office the central government would cease to exist and the nation would perish.[26] Barely two months after the close of the Washington Conference, war broke out between the two military cliques. Chang's armies were beaten by Wu and withdrawn beyond the Great Wall; Liang and subsequently President Hsu were overthrown.

Whatever might have developed internally, the fact remains that the Chinese delegates in Washington, never having received instructions to the contrary, continued on their present course of action. It is not surprising that when conversations resumed on January 4, 1922, the Japanese attitude hardened perceptibly. Both sides discreetly refrained from divulging what information their home governments had sent them in regard to the interview. Sze regretted this lack of confidence on the part of his Japanese colleagues, while Shidehara thought it only natural that the Japanese minister should inquire of the new cabinet whether its policy would be different from that of the outgoing cabinet concerning the railway loan agreement.[27] Coming to the subject matter, Koo, concerned about the reported personal commitment of Premier Liang, left no doubt that not only the Chinese delegates personally were unable to see the wisdom of accepting a Japanese loan as the best

18

means for payment, but the instructions from the Chinese Government had made it perfectly clear that he and his colleagues ought not to go beyond the two alternative Chinese plans. Shidehara retorted, not without a touch of sarcasm, that he had of course no knowledge of what instructions his Chinese colleagues had received from home, but that his instructions were quite explicit. His delegation had to insist upon the plan for a railway loan agreement.

The sixth of January was a fateful day. The Japanese delegation, as Koo observed, took a step backward in abruptly reverting to the plan for a Japanese loan. Shidehara indicated that they had never abandoned it. The two delegations were thus approaching an *impasse*. With the Liang-Obata interview fresh in mind, Shidehara suggested to the Chinese delegation that they should refer the matter to Peking. Whereupon Koo reaffirmed the position of the home government, "without wishing unnecessarily," he stressed, "to interest the Japanese delegates in China's politics."[28]

To break this deadlock the Chinese delegation sought to invoke the good offices of Hughes and Balfour. The Japanese disagreed. Shidehara pointed out that his instructions from Tokyo were so explicit regarding the matter at issue that the Japanese delegation was not in a position to solicit good offices. In reply, Koo said the Chinese delegates understood that the conversations had been entered upon because of the availability of these good offices. This offer they regarded as continuous and therefore available at any time. As Shidehara stood firm, Koo suggested that observers, Hughes and Balfour, be invited to attend the next meeting. The Japanese delegate did not object to their presence, but said that giving good offices at the request of one party alone would amount to intervention. This incident unmistakably indicated the Japanese attitude toward the function of the observers. The deadlock was complete.

The 20th meeting adjourned *sine die* and the two delegations issued a joint communiqué. An abridged version of this communiqué will serve to summarize their positions at that time.

The Japanese Plan

The Japanese delegates proposed a railway loan agreement plan on the basis of the terms of ordinary railway loan agreements entered into by China with various foreign capitalists during recent years: (a) Term to be fifteen years with option of redemption after five years; (b) A Japanese traffic manager and a Japanese chief accountant; (c) Details to be worked out in Peking.

The Chinese Alternatives

China's two alternative plans: (1) Cash payment with a single deposit in a bank of a third Power at a specified date; (2) Deferred payment in treasury notes or notes of the Chinese Bankers Union, over a period of twelve years, with option of redemption after three years. China to select and employ a Japanese district engineer.

The proposal of either side was unacceptable to the other.

While the Sino-Japanese conversations turned to other matters, Hughes and Balfour spared no effort behind the stage to explore the possibility of a compromise on the railway issue. The two observers, MacMurray and Lampson, suggested, on their personal responsibility, four alternative bases for compromise. These were communicated by the two delegations to their governments for consideration. The contacts these two diplomats had with the Chinese delegates were particularly relaxed since they often took place late in the evenings at the Legation and at Koo's residence at Moran House. They served the purpose of developing and essaying ideas rather than establishing positions—"less like ordinary diplomatic negotiations than like what college undergraduates would call bull-sessions."[29] Mac-

Murray and Lampson were advisers on Far Eastern affairs keeping their superiors well acquainted with the political atmosphere, the trends, and the inside stories of the conversations.

Hughes and Balfour jointly arranged separate informal talks with the two delegations.[30] During the interview with the Japanese delegates on January 18 at Balfour's apartment in Washington, the two English-speaking statesmen acceded to what the Japanese considered to be their maximum concession. This was done in order to induce the Japanese to agree to the settlement of the Shantung question, without which the conference would be a failure. It remained for the two gentlemen to have the Japanese formula transmitted to the Chinese. The principal features were

... *deferred payment by Chinese treasury notes running for fifteen years, but redeemable at any time after five years; appointment of a Japanese chief accountant, and of a Chinese chief accountant, of coequal powers, both of them subject to the control of the Chinese director-general of the railway; and appointment of a Japanese traffic manager subject to the control of the Chinese director-general* . . .[31]

After the interview with the Japanese delegates, Hughes and Balfour had two interviews with the three Chinese delegates, one on January 19 and the other on January 22 both at Hughes's home. The American Secretary of State said in substance that the Japanese, having actual possession of Kiaochow and the railway, could not be compelled to withdraw except by force if an agreement were not reached; that Japan, having receded from the original position of joint enterprise of the railway, had in fact made large concessions to China; that questions of a technical nature should not be allowed to stand in the way of a settlement; and that the situation was serious. The moment had arrived for reaching a decision by choosing between compliance with Japan's last offer and an irretrievable loss of

Shantung. The British leader expressed similar views. Arguments advanced by the Chinese visitors, including the one that the Chinese had 37,000,000 people in Shantung against 20,000 Japanese and that this should entitle China to the management of the railway, did not make much impression upon the listeners. These points were brushed aside as insignificant and negligible in comparison with the larger and more important issues at stake. Balfour begged his Chinese friends to exercise some sense of proportion, pointing out that five years was a short time in the average life of a man, and was inconsiderable in comparison with the life of a nation, particularly a nation with a history as long as that of China. It was incredible, he stressed, that all that China stood to gain should be frustrated by a technical appointment on a railway in which only a period of five years was involved.

The reasons which led the American and British leaders to urge the Chinese government to accept this proposed solution were fully and frankly set forth in a cable which Hughes dispatched on January 22 to the American Minister in China, Jacob G. Schurman. The essential paragraphs of this document are excerpted here: [32]

. . . *Mr. Balfour and I have discussed the Shantung question with both Chinese and Japanese delegations, and very earnestly explored the possibilities of settlement. We have been forcibly impressed with the fact that, whatever the merits of the several issues involved, the situation requires that both Powers concerned must act on the realization that no ideal or academic solution is possible and that they must be prepared without further delay to accept a reasonable, practical basis of compromise as the only alternative to a failure of negotiations which would aggravate the question and place it beyond the possibility of adjustment for an indefinite period. This necessity rests the more heavily on China because of the fact that the conduct of these negotiations in the atmosphere of the Conference affords an op-*

22

portunity such as cannot be expected to recur for obtaining Japan's relinquishment of the position which she now holds in Shantung; and the fact that any settlement now arrived at would be reported to the Conference and taken cognizance of by it would afford the highest sanction for an agreement reached at this time . . .

You will very earnestly impress upon Doctor Yen the conviction, which is fully shared by Mr. Balfour and myself, that this arrangement represents the final limit to which Japan is prepared to go and which China must be prepared to accept as the only available means of realizing the hope of reestablishing herself in Shantung within the foreseeable future . . .

. . . although the American delegates fully respect the effort of China to secure the best possible terms, they all consider the points remaining at issue to be of such little importance compared with the other interests at stake that any degree of toleration with regard to a refusal by the Chinese to meet the practical situation which confronts them now would not be justified. You may add that I have the President's authority for stating this to be the attitude of our Government. Various American expressions of sympathy with an academic position may have misled the Chinese. Before deciding against such a settlement the Chinese should realize that if they choose to break off negotiations on the relatively unimportant issues outstanding and thus bring upon themselves the disasters which may be expected, they cannot count on any support either from public sentiment in the United States or from this Government . . .

At Sze's request, Hughes took him to see President Harding on January 25. Harding told Sze that it would be a colossal blunder in statecraft if China were not to take advantage of the opportunity now offered her for the settlement of the Shantung question. The alternative might involve losing the province.[33]

The American Minister Schurman acted with tact, energy, and good judgment. His handling of the matter earned for him a tribute of appreciation from his superior, the Secretary of State. In like manner, the British Minister in Peking, Beilby F. Alston, played his part well. As a result of all these developments, the Chinese government, under the wise leadership of President Hsu and his Foreign Minister and Acting Premier, W. W. Yen, notwithstanding some strong opposition and the ensuing Cabinet crisis, decided to accept the terms. Instructions were issued to the delegation to that effect. In fact, Yen thought that the terms were better than could have been expected either by the President or by himself. In some quarters, however, there existed an impression that the American and British governments had exerted heavy pressure on the Peking government or on its delegates in Washington to induce them to accept a settlement unfavorable to China.

As a finishing touch to all these diplomatic activities that had taken place outside the conference room, there was an interview between Hughes and Balfour on the one hand and the three Chinese delegates on the other, at the house of the Secretary of State, during the morning of January 30. Sze remarked that China's consent to appoint Japanese officials should not interfere with her aspiration for the unification of the Chinese railways. Hughes intervened by saying that he hardly saw the pertinency of the remark. Hughes rather stressed the need for a prompt settlement which should not be delayed by reason of small details. Toward the close of the talk, Koo summed up the Chinese position as follows: The Chinese delegation wanted the Japanese traffic manager to carry out and be bound by the general regulations governing the administration of Chinese-government railways. By expressing the hope that the conversations would be resumed and that they would try as best they could to arrive at an agreement on that basis, the Chinese representatives virtually accepted the formula.

When both sides met again in the conference room to

discuss the railway question in the afternoon of January 30, the only thing they had to do was to compare the notes of the talks they had had separately with the two intermediaries, and to find in their briefcases the agreed formula which had simply to be put in the proper form of a treaty stipulation. Since both parties gave their assent to it, the formula found its way into the Shantung treaty.

There remained only a few more items for settlement. However, an unexpectedly protracted debate ensued on the question of the subordinate staff of the two Japanese officials. This was finally settled by a Japanese declaration that Japan had no intention of claiming that China was under any obligation to appoint Japanese nationals as members of the subordinate staff. The meeting on that day was the longest, lasting from three in the afternoon until ten in the evening.

The Shantung conversations thus came to a successful close. The agreement had covered all the points at issue: the restoration of Kiaochow, the transfer of the railway, the restitution of other economic rights, the renunciation of preferential rights, the withdrawal of Japanese troops, and other matters. The two delegations then communicated separately to the United States Secretary of State the substance of the terms agreed upon. On February 1, Hughes read the Shantung agreement at the Fifth Plenary Session of the Conference and caused it to be put into the record. As stated before, the agreement was signed by the Chinese and Japanese plenipotentiaries on February 4, and it was signed in the presence of Hughes and Balfour at the Pan American Union Building. Indeed, the presence of these two gentlemen at the opening of the Sino-Japanese conversations and at the signing of the Shantung treaty lent a particular authority and significance to the proceedings.

At the same plenary session, after the Shantung agreement had been reported to the Conference, Balfour announced that the British Government was now ready to surrender the lease of Weihaiwei to China.

In concluding this chapter on Shantung, it is fitting to reproduce a telegram[34] which the President of the United States received on February 5 from the President of China:

I am most happy to learn that during the Conference at Washington, through the untiring friendly interest taken by Your Excellency and by all the American Delegates, a solution of the long outstanding Shantung question has been made possible. Thus the peace of the Far East is further ensured. On behalf of the Government and people of the Republic of China, I have the honor to extend to Your Excellency our sincere thanks and felicitations.

As provided for in the Shantung treaty, the Japanese troops stationed along the Tsingtao-Tsinanfu railway began their withdrawal prior to its coming into force; this withdrawal was completed in May 1922. The treaty became effective in June. Headed by C. T. Wang for China and Obata for Japan, the Joint Commission formed under the treaty was able to wind up its work by an agreement signed on December 1. This agreement covered the details left over by the Shantung treaty, with the exception of railway questions. These were dealt with by the Joint Railway Commission under the leadership of Wang and Obata. In the meantime the Kiaochow Leased Territory had been transferred from Japan to China sometime in October, while the port of Tsingtao was handed back one month later. On December 5 the commissioners signed another agreement by which the details relative to the transfer of the railway and the valuation of its properties were settled. By the end of the year the last Japanese troops left Tsingtao.

The formal transfer of the railway took place on January 1, 1923. The railway properties included the main line itself, its branches, wharves, warehouses, and similar properties. Their value had been originally assessed by the Reparations Commission at Paris to be 53,400,000 gold marks; it was now fixed by the Sino-Japanese Commission at 40,000,000 Japanese Yen, roughly corresponding to

$19,000,000 in U.S. currency. The railroad was transferred to China against the delivery to the Japanese government of "The Treasury Notes of the Tsingtao-Tsinanfu Railway," at par value, bearing an annual interest of six per cent payable semi-annually. A Japanese traffic manager and a Japanese chief accountant were selected and appointed by the Chinese government pending the redemption of the notes. An early attempt was made to transform the railway into a joint stock company through public subscriptions, in the hope that when sufficient funds were raised, the right of option could be exercised, the notes redeemed at the end of five years, and the services of the Japanese officials dispensed with. The plan, however, did not materialize mainly because of unsettled political conditions in China and partly because of the lack of enthusiasm on the part of the public.[35] Despite some arrears, all interest payments were made up to and including the month of June 1937, but no payment having been made towards amortisation, the indebtedness was eventually cancelled by the war and the peace treaty between China and Japan.[36]

The Nine Power Treaty
Relating to Principles and Policies Concerning China

It was to be regretted that on the eve of and during the Washington Conference China did not find herself in a position to give a more encouraging account of her domestic conditions before the bar of world opinion.[37] Canton claimed to be the constitutional government thereby contesting the legitimacy of the very government which had been invited to take part in the conference. The central government, however, could hardly make its voice listened to beyond the confines of the capital of Peking. The provinces or their coalitions formed practically a collection of principalities or kingdoms within the empire, a sort of *imperium in imperio*. The *tuchuns*, that is, provincial war lords, either professed loyalty to the Peking government or else openly defied its authority. They continued to fight one another. For years the civil war in China had been alternating between an uneasy peace and sporadic outbreaks. A civil war, too, has its cold and hot phases. Nothing illustrates this point more clearly and more poignantly than the tragic developments surrounding the Liang-Obata interview as stated above. But neither the pen nor the sword on either side was sufficiently mighty to bring the others to such terms as to impose a definite military and political decision. The hordes of troops, totalling no less than a million in number according to one estimate, were maintained by the war lords for their own purposes. They by no means constituted an army in the modern sense of the word. What was worse, these regiments or divisions of troops, and for that matter the few antiquated warships too, not infrequently served as instruments for the sale or transfer of allegiance. Moreover, it was precisely the maintenance of this huge army which caused a heavy drain on the national treasury. The central government, thus deprived of substantial sources of revenue, had to rely more and more on foreign loans to meet its administrative expenses with all the undesirable consequences flowing from this arrangement. As a matter of fact, the government defaulted on certain foreign loan payments[38] at the moment of the convening of the Conference, which was the worst thing that could have befallen China insofar as propaganda was concerned. In an editorial entitled "Preparations for Washington," the London *Times* of October 24, 1921, said: "China, from the point of view of international relations, is, in her present divided state, largely a fiction." However exaggerated and even insinuating the statement might be, there was unfortunately a certain amount of truth in it.

Despite these circumstances the Chinese delegates came to the conference table in a hopeful mood, though not without a good deal of apprehension and skepticism. It was hoped that the Conference would do something to remove or loosen at least a part of the then existing limitations upon China's freedom of action. At the same time it was also feared that advantage might be taken of the troubled conditions in the country to aggravate encroachments on her sovereign rights. In the midst of this awkward dilemma, the delegation naturally felt impelled to work out and bring forward a concrete program of principles at the first opportunity. These feelings were shared by China's friends too, notably the United States and the British Empire, which also recognized the need and usefulness of formulating certain guiding principles to govern their relations, and those of other powers, with China. Their purpose, as will be seen, was rather to preserve the *status quo* than to introduce a new chapter of international relations in regard to China; rather to regulate the future conduct than to redress past grievances she might have had against other powers; in a word, to attempt to improve the existing situation by preventing its deterioration. The principles thus enunciated were by no means a novelty. But this was the first time that they were made into a multilateral commitment. Take, for instance, the principle of the "open door." That principle and its counterpart, the integrity of the Chinese Empire, owed their inception to the unilateral declarations which were initiated by the United States government. Favorable responses were made by the interested powers some sixty years ago. Later they were embodied in a number of bilateral agreements. Finally they were enshrined in the multilateral treaty of Washington.

The British Chief Delegate was the first, on the eve of the Conference, to prepare and informally to present to Hughes a draft treaty to be considered and concluded between the British Empire, China, France, Japan, and the United States.[39] Known as the "Balfour draft," this personal memorandum consisted of six articles. The objectives were: (a) the consolidation and maintenance of the general peace in Eastern Asia, (b) the preservation of the independence and integrity of the Chinese Republic, (c) the application of the principle of equal opportunity for the commerce and industry of all nations in China, and (d) the substitution of international co-operation for international rivalry in China. It was to propose, among other things, that the five governments would, whenever any one of these principles was in jeopardy, communicate with one another fully and frankly. They would in common consider measures to be taken to safeguard their menaced rights or interests. Although this draft had never been laid before the Conference, most of the underlying ideas were incorporated in the final treaty, though not the one suggesting joint consideration of measures in the event of a crisis.

At the first meeting of the Pacific and Far Eastern Committee, held on November 16, 1921, Sze presented on behalf of the Chinese delegation the now celebrated ten points.[40] The most essential features were (a) respect for the territorial integrity of China, (b) application of the Open Door policy to all of China, (c) removal, "immediately or as soon as circumstances will permit," of existing limitations upon China's political, jurisdictional and administrative freedom of action, and (d) provision for the peaceful settlement of international disputes in the Pacific and Far East, and for the holding of future conferences to discuss international questions affecting that region. In his introductory statement, the Chinese chief delegate had this to say:

China is now contending with certain difficult problems which necessarily arise when any country makes a radical change in her form of government. These problems she will be able to solve if given the opportunity to do so. This means not only that she should be freed from the danger or threat of foreign aggression, but that, so far as circumstances will possibly permit, she be relieved from limitations which now deprive her of autonomous administrative action and prevent her from securing adequate public revenues.

A preliminary exchange of views took place in the committee with reference to the Chinese proposals. Elihu Root was, at his own suggestion, entrusted with the task of formulating the various principles in a single resolution for further examination.[41] One point which had emerged from the brief discussions of the Chinese program, however, deserves attention.[42] It happened that the French Premier and chief delegate, Aristide Briand, speaking about the principle of territorial integrity of China, indicated that the principle in question had significance only if a definition of the boundaries of China were first determined upon, in view of the fact that France had a common frontier with China of about 1,500 kilometers in length. But when it came to Root's turn to express his views, he quite accidentally referred to the French delegate's remark as being in the form of an inquiry: "What is China?" Doubtless laboring under a misconception, Root indicated that in his opinion distinction should be made between China proper and the territories over which China exercised suzerainty, and that the resolution he was to prepare should at the first stage be limited in its application to China proper. This suggestion was dropped after Koo had explained that according to the Chinese constitution the Republic of China included China proper and the outlying territories. The incident was thus closed, but the press, as will be shown later in this paper,[43] seized upon this occasion to put into the mouth of the French statesman some unfriendly words concerning China and the delegation, words which he had not uttered.

Elihu Root was the author not only of the resolution embodying the four clauses associated with his name but likewise of the treaty in its entirety. This treaty was also known as the Open Door Treaty, inasmuch as it went into some details in its stipulations for the fair and effective application of that long established principle. The four clauses were submitted by Root for discussion during the third meeting of the Committee on November 21st.[44] But it seemed that they did not receive much attention from the participating delegations. The discussions were completed in the course of one session. This session lasted for barely two hours, mainly because the draft document, with one exception to be mentioned shortly, represented an endeavour to gather together what had been accepted by all the powers including China. Incidentally, it had not even been shown to any representative of the most directly interested power—China—prior to its presentation, nor did the Chinese delegates ask for an extended discussion. The four principles, as finally adopted by the Conference, were as follows:

The Contracting Powers, other than China, agree:

(1) To respect the sovereignty, the independence, and the territorial and administrative integrity of China;

(2) To provide the fullest and most unembarrassed opportunity to China to develop and maintain for herself an effective and stable government;

(3) To use their influence for the purpose of effectually establishing and maintaining the principle of equal opportunity for the commerce and industry of all nations throughout the territory of China;

(4) To refrain from taking advantage of conditions in China in order to seek special rights or privileges which would abridge the rights of subjects or citizens of friendly States and from countenancing action inimical to the security of such States.

While the first three principles do not need any comment, the import and the origin and significance of the fourth should be examined fully. Obviously concerned about its purpose and implications, Koo sought clarification, saying that while the draft resolution would take the *status quo* as a point of departure, it was not intended to maintain and still less to perpetuate the existing conditions in impairment of China's sovereign rights. Hughes replied by pointing out that those would be particular questions. Curious about the word "security" in the latter part of the fourth clause, Balfour quite innocently said he wondered how the security of any state would be affected but did not press the point after an explanation was given by the chairman. The explanatory remarks did not appear in the official minutes.

A careful study of the matter reveals that the principle in question, in its two parts, was of Japanese origin. It will be recalled that in the formation of the Four-Power-Group Consortium for foreign loans to China,[45] in the years 1918-1920, Japan urged the exclusion of certain regions of Manchuria and Mongolia from the scope of the pooling arrangements on the alleged grounds that the national and economic security of Japan depended on those regions. After a long and stubborn diplomatic struggle between Japan and the three other powers (U.S.A., Britain, and France), she withdrew the demand, having obtained formal assurances from the three powers that the Consortium would not undertake any operations prejudicial to the economic life and national defense of Japan and that in any case such operations would not be countenanced by the other three governments concerned. W. W. Willoughby was correct in pointing out that "one sees in this language a possible source of some of the words of the fourth Resolution adopted by the Conference."[46] He was equally correct in stating[47] that this particular clause was not based, as were the other three, "upon statements previously made in the Committee by the several Delegations"; that in fact Root "had received no specific instruction from the Committee to frame and introduce it"; and that the proposition "was initiated by the American delegation upon its own responsibility." It is, however, difficult to understand how its adoption could, as Willoughby added, mean "a decisive victory" for China, seeing that she had persistently taken exception to Japan's claim to exclusive privileges in the regions indicated above. Again, as for the first part of the clause under review—that is, no abridgment of the rights of other states—it was actually a reaffirmation of the secret promise which had been made by Japan as part of the Lansing-Ishii agreement of 1917.[48] It is therefore clear that the two parts of this clause were designed to counterbalance one another with the object of confirming the Japanese position in Manchuria in return for safeguarding the vested rights of other powers in China.

Hardly three weeks after the opening of the Conference, it became widely known that sharp internal differences had arisen within the Chinese delegation. A few members of the staff felt uneasy and unhappy, partly because of the hurried manner in which the ten-point program was drawn up and brought before the Committee, and possibly also because of alleged pressure from the English-speaking delegates upon the Chinese delegation for compromise.[49] There were also other complicating factors which consisted, for instance, in the circulation of conflicting reports by the "people's delegates" and by Sun Yat-sen's personal representative in Washington. As a result, the Secretary General of the delegation, Philip K. C. Tyau, resigned. A few others, including C. H. Wang, likewise offered or threatened resignation. These unpleasant developments caused Hughes so much concern that he instructed the American Minister in Peking to use his discretion, "as a suitable occasion offers," to make clear to the Chinese government that if the support of Sze and Koo should be withdrawn and if they should thereby be compelled to abandon an attitude of helpfulness and conciliation for one of uncompromising obstruction, the result "would be to dissipate the sympathy and confidence they have thus far commanded, and react very unfavorably upon the work of the Conference in general and more particularly upon China's position." The Envoy carried out his instructions when one day he saw W. W. Yen, Foreign Minister, at a flood-relief ball in the Foreign Office. He was given the reassuring reply that the Chinese government would support the two delegates.[50] In retrospect, the arguments advanced in opposition to some of China's ten points and to America's four principles were as sound in theory as they were unrealistic in practice. The dissenting members contended that it was derogatory to an independent state to seek a guarantee of independence from other states and that the open door principle was but a misnomer to camouflage the plan of joint aggression of all foreign powers against China.[51]

Whatever the views held in regard to the Nine Power Treaty, academic or practical, the important thing was to know whether its provisions were efficacious when the moment came for their application, or, in other words, whether the treaty could stand the test of the inexorable march of events. Let us therefore recall briefly the events which unfolded in the years following the conclusion of that international instrument. No sooner had the National government been established in Nanking to organize itself for the tasks of unification and stabilization than Japan staged the Tsinan incident. That incident opened the long chapter of Japanese aggressions against her neighbour culminating in the outbreak of full-scale hostilities at Loukouchiao only nine miles southwest of Peiping. Thus Japan denied China the opportunity to develop and maintain for herself an effective and stable government; she infringed upon the sovereignty, independence, and territorial and administrative integrity of China; she disregarded the principle of the open door in any part of China that was brought under her domination or occupation; in a word, she violated all the international treaties including the Nine Power Treaty and the Paris Peace Pact of 1928. Last but not least Japan ignored the Covenant of the League of Nations and withdrew from the organization. The League proved itself absolutely powerless to call a halt to her aggressions.

The Nine Power Conference was convened in Brussels in November 1937 to deal with the grave situation in the Far East. Japan refused to attend despite two invitations. The Brussels Conference in which nineteen nations participated[52] shared the same fate as the world organization in

Geneva; nothing emerged from the Conference save a full and frank exchange of views among the participating delegations regarding the crisis. It was a failure, and so was the treaty of Washington of February 6, 1922.

The Nine Power Treaty Relating to Chinese Customs Tariff

Finding herself constantly in financial embarrassment and naturally jealous of her sovereign rights, China attached great importance to the inclusion and discussion of the questions of Chinese customs tariff with a view to an early restoration of tariff autonomy. When China suggested, on October 19, 1921, a tentative agenda for the coming conference to be convened three weeks later, the conspicuous omission of the Shantung question as such in the proposed list was matched by the equally conspicuous introduction of the item of tariff autonomy.[53] Again, on November 5, in a conversation with Hughes, Sze, the principal Chinese delegate, specifically expressed the wish of the Chinese Government to bring up the tariff question. He obtained confirmation of his understanding that this could be done under the heading of administrative integrity of China.[54] Then, when presenting China's program of ten points, as narrated above, he stated clearly that China should be relieved, as far as circumstances permitted, from "limitations which now deprive her of autonomous administrative action and prevent her from securing adequate public revenues." The item of customs tariff was included in the proposals by which China's administrative independence was to be respected and the restrictions on her administrative freedom of action were to be removed.

On November 23, at the fifth meeting of the Pacific and Far Eastern Committee, Koo presented China's case on customs tariff.[55] Having given a brief historical account of the tariff, he claimed the right to tariff autonomy on the ground that the then existing customs regime in China constituted not only an infringement of her sovereign right but also a serious impediment to her economic development. This rendered it impossible for her to make reciprocity arrangements with other countries. It also failed to take into consideration the economic, fiscal, and social needs of China. The Chinese government, however, had no desire to disturb the existing customs administration nor to interfere with the allocation of the revenue to the payment of foreign loans secured on it. But as the establishment of a new regime would require time, it should come into force only after a period to be agreed upon. In the meantime, a maximum rate should be agreed to, so that China could, within the limits imposed by that rate, enjoy freedom of fixing and differentiating rates, for example, between luxuries and necessaries. For this purpose it was proposed that on and from January 1, 1922, the Chinese import tariff should be raised to 12½ per cent—a rate mentioned in the Chinese treaties of 1902 and 1903 with Great Britain, the United States and Japan.

After a preliminary discussion during which the views and suggestions made by the Chinese delegate were by no means favorably entertained, a sub-committee was formed to examine the matter further in all its aspects.

In an editorial entitled "China at the Conference," the London *Times* of November 26, 1921, started with these astounding words: ". . . until the Conference makes up its mind as to 'what is China' no progress is possible towards a settlement of the Far Eastern question." Commenting on Koo's statement in the Committee, the editorial continued: "Mr. Koo is a brilliant instance of the results of Western education as applied to an adaptable Chinese intellect. His English is faultless, and this speech, if it stood alone, would suffice to show how completely he has mastered the art of employing Western catchwords in the manner best calculated to play upon popular opinion." The address was construed to be a "dexterous attack upon the Chinese Maritime Customs." Koo began, the *Times* went on to say, "by protesting that nothing could be farther from the mind of his Government. Yet it must be owned that

. . . the trend of his arguments, and even his specific demands, do seem to imply a desire to undermine the Customs, if not to destroy them. The Imperial Maritime Customs have rendered invaluable services to both the Government and the people of China for a great number of years. They have saved her from bankruptcy and from the dangers which bankruptcy must have brought upon her at the hands of creditors, some of whom would have known how to utilize her default for the attainment of objects they would have greatly preferred to the regular payment of interest upon their advances. The Customs, at the same time, have been a check upon the corruption and venality which for centuries have been the recognized prerogatives of Chinese officialdom.

The Maritime Customs and later the Salt Gabelle, so the London paper continued to explain, "have been the chief checks upon domestic corruption and foreign rapacity, in the interests of the Chinese people . . ." The editorial concluded:

The apparent anxiety of the Chinese delegates at Washington to destroy or to emasculate a system which worked admirably in the past, and set an example of pure and honest administration in the interests of the people, naturally gives rise to doubts and questionings among persons acquainted with Far Eastern affairs. The French delegates[56] gave expression to some of these doubts by bluntly asking Mr. Koo and his colleagues on what authority they affect to speak for China as a whole, at a time when it is notorious that the feeble Government at Peking exercises no power and little influence over a great part of the eighteen provinces, not to say anything of the other parts of the Empire. The answer that the Government of Peking is the only recognized government in China does not meet the inquiry.

38

The matter of real moment to the Conference and to the world is not what the Mandarins in Peking, or what the Western educated reformers in the South, desire, but what the people of China—the dumb, industrious peaceful millions of China—desire. It is thought that, like most other peoples, their chief aspiration is to secure some semblance of good and honest government, and it is questioned whether they greatly concern themselves about the realization of the high ideals of national sovereignty eloquently and adroitly proclaimed by Mr. Koo. That the Mandarins would like to have the handling of the large sums receivable by the Customs is undoubted; that the people would care to see it in their hands is very doubtful indeed. The eloquence of the Chinese delegates may delude the uninformed; it can only serve to remind those who know Asiatics that the more an Oriental diplomatist is Westernized the less confidence does he command in the East.

The editorial extracted above was a frank statement of views, but it showed a total lack of sympathy with China's struggle for democracy and for equality. It reflected the policy of most of the powers toward China as well as general public opinion in the West: to cling desperately to their vested interests regardless of the rights and interests of China. It refused not only to acknowledge the justice of her claim to customs autonomy but also to study the signs of the changing times. Lastly, the unkind remarks directed against Western-educated diplomats of China was wholly uncalled for. To imply that demand for customs tariff autonomy did not represent the unanimous wish of the Chinese people was untrue, to say the least. It should be added, however, that many great daily newspapers, by limiting their attention to the realities of the hour, have not forfeited their usefulness through the passage of time. The editorial of the hour may still serve to provide thinking statesmen with food for serious thought in handling future problems of national and international significance.

The Sub-Committee on Chinese Revenue held its first meeting on November 29, 1921. It had six meetings in all. The last meeting was held on January 4 in the following year. Oscar W. Underwood, minority leader of the U. S. Senate, was its chairman. China was represented by Koo. At the first meeting Koo brought forward six specific proposals,[57] which were designed to spell out what he had outlined and explained in the Committee of the Whole. The proposals consisted of a series of stages beginning with the immediate increase of the customs schedule to 12½ per cent, abolition of *likin*,[58] and the simultaneous levy of certain surtaxes, to be followed by the establishment of a new treaty regime for a short period of time, leading finally to the abrogation of all treaties relating to customs tariff and other related matters at the end of ten years from date of agreement.

No mention, however, was made of the revision of the tariff schedule from the actual rate of 3½ per cent to the treaty rate of 5 per cent effective.[59] This was a matter which from the Chinese point of view was taken for granted and which therefore did not require any proposal for its implementation. But this was the only point on which a unanimous agreement could be obtained at that time. Even discussion of the treaty stipulations relating to surtaxes in return for the abolition of *likin* also involved obstacles. The alleged reason was the length of time it would take to put them into execution. In short, there was a general reluctance on the part of the foreign powers to see China's customs revenue actually increased to any considerable extent, for fear, as it was pointed out, that owing to the disturbing conditions then obtaining in China and the lack of a parliamentary government, the increased revenues might be absorbed to a very great extent by the provincial military governors instead of going to the central government. They might thus be used to cause further disturbance in China rather than to improve China's general administration and to promote the welfare of the people. The possibility of restoration of tariff autonomy immediately or in the foreseeable future was virtually ruled out from the very beginning.

During the early stages of deliberation, however, the English-speaking delegates made an honest, though indeed modest, effort to meet some of China's wishes. On November 30, at the second meeting of the Sub-Committee, Robert Borden, speaking for the British Empire,[60] suggested an immediate revision to 5 per cent effective and another revision to follow in four years. He proposed to raise the rate to 7½ per cent on the basis of the schedule resulting from this succeeding revision, with an additional increase on certain specified articles of luxury. On behalf of the Japanese delegation, Masunosuké Odagiri, a bank director and former delegate for the conclusion of the Sino-Japanese commercial treaty of 1903, read a statement declaring it impossible to accept the proposed net increase of 2½ per cent. The reason he gave was that this sudden and big increase would have a serious effect on the industry of Japan. It would also force higher prices on purchasers in China. The proposal was, however, accepted by Koo and then by all other delegations except the Japanese. When asked by the chairman whether the Japanese representative had further views to express in the face of the overwhelming support of the Borden proposition, he paused for a moment, picked up the same statement, and once more read it slowly and in a low voice. This done, silence took possession of the committee room for a few seconds. The British proposal was thus vetoed by the Japanese delegate during that meeting. The chairman adjourned the meeting subject to his call.[61] (I have personally noted in this connection that Japanese diplomats at international conferences seldom hesitate to talk in an over-cautious manner, or to confess ignorance of a delicate point. They frequently wish to refer the matter to a Japanese expert or to seek fresh instructions from their government. The hesitancy of the Japanese diplomats apparently contrasts with, but, in fact,

41

matches well, the alertness of their Chinese counterparts.)

During the interval which lasted about a month, Borden had separate informal talks with Koo and the Japanese representative as well as with the chairman in an effort to reconcile the opposing views and to bring about unanimity. As a result, the British representative was able to present to the Sub-Committee as a basis for discussion a draft agreement by which a future conference was to be called to take care of all problems that might be left over by the Washington Conference. That was how the Special Conference idea came into the picture. It was a typical pass-the-buck tactic so commonly practiced in international affairs. In a sub-committee or a drafting committee, the task is to devise a formula which sidetracks the controversy and leads the conference to a satisfactory conclusion along the line of least resistance. The formula in this case was to do one thing at present and to leave everything else to the future. That one thing was of course the immediate revision of the import tariff on the basis of five per cent effective. Then a special conference was to be convened in the future, among other things, to authorize the levying of a surtax on dutiable imports, at a uniform rate of $2\frac{1}{2}$ per cent with another increase on certain articles of luxury, "as from such date, for such purposes, and subject to such conditions as it (i.e., the Special Conference) may determine."

The phrase "for such purposes" did not appear in the Borden draft but was subsequently inserted in the final text of the treaty so as to give satisfaction to the insistent demands of the French delegate. The fact was that in the Sub-Committee Koo had a difficult time in resisting the attempts made by the Japanese and French delegates to open up the discussion of the uses to which the increased customs revenues were to be devoted. In this respect the English-speaking delegates and others were more polite and more moderate in tone. It was the Japanese delegate who initiated the idea that the additional revenue should first be used for the service of foreign loans.[62] Then Kammerer, a minister plenipotentiary and a member of the French delegation, who had previously served on the commissions for the revision of the Chinese customs tariffs, followed it up by formally suggesting to include in the text the following words: that "the increase in revenue derived from the increase in customs duties" should be "pledged primarily to the service of the foreign loans guaranteed by the customs receipts, when the latter are insufficient, as well as for the reimbursement of the matured bonds of the Chinese Treasury, payment of which has been suspended."[63] In spite of Koo's objection and of the explanatory remarks made by a few other delegates, the French representative insisted upon his amendment, indicating that there were already two or three loans in default. Thereupon Koo reminded him that the Chinese government funds tied up in a French bank called the Banque Industrielle de Chine which had recently failed had amounted to more than China's debt to France.[64] As a compromise, the words "for such purposes" were used in the final text. It was this Frenchman who warned more than once that ratification of the treaty was essential to the carrying out of its provisions.

Another delicate matter had arisen in connection with the question of the seat of the future conference. The Sub-Committee of Nine on Drafting under Elihu Root's chairmanship was putting finishing touches to the treaty when a discussion on that point took place.[65] It appeared that the original draft provided that the conference be held in Peking within three months after the ratification of the treaty. The Netherlands delegate, Jonkheer Beelaerts van Blokland, preferred Shanghai to Peking, because in Shanghai accurate information concerning trade conditions and market prices of goods could be more easily collected. The Chairman said that Peking was chosen because some place had to be chosen, and also because in Peking the diplomatic representatives were on the spot to make arrangements with the help of the Chinese Foreign Office. Sir Auckland

43

Geddes of the British delegation saw some reason in the Netherlands suggestion, and added that at any rate the special conference was to be held on Chinese soil and that therefore it would be better to leave the matter in the hands of the Chinese Government. Possibly recalling the contact he had previously had with Ma Soo, Dr. Sun Yat-sen's personal representative in Washington, Root made the remark that Peking and Canton might compete with each other to be the seat of the conference. It was this remark which provoked some laughter among those present. At Koo's suggestion, it was finally agreed to substitute the word "China" for "Peking" so that the choice of a place together with that of a date would, in accordance with international usage, be entrusted to the judgment of the convening power in consultation with other participating powers.

In giving his assent to the resolution by which Underwood presented the Tariff Treaty to the full Committee for adoption at its 17th meeting held on January 5, 1922, Koo made a statement[66] regarding the re-establishment of tariff autonomy—a matter, he emphasized, to which the Chinese people attached extreme importance. He energetically defended the demand made by China for early restoration of the customs tariff autonomy on political, fiscal, economic, social and moral grounds. The speech was most eloquent and appealing. He concluded: ". . . the Chinese delegation feel in duty bound to declare that . . . it is not their desire, in assenting to the agreement now before you, to relinquish their claim (for the restoration of tariff autonomy) ; on the contrary, it is their intention to bring the question up again for consideration on all appropriate occasions in the future." This lengthy, important document is textually reproduced as an appendix to this present monograph.

Having heard Koo's statement, Underwood had this to say: So far as he was concerned, he gladly welcomed an

44

opportunity of restoring to China her entire fiscal autonomy. ... He felt sure, he added, that—

when China herself established a parliamentary government of all the Provinces of China and dispensed with the military control that now existed in many of the Provinces of China, so that the outside Powers might feel that they were dealing with a government that had entire and absolute and free control of the situation, China could expect to realize the great ideals of sovereignty that she asked for at this table.[67]

In the opinion of the Democratic Senator, however, the customs tariff treaty being in the nature of a trade agreement, it could be denounced by China in certain contingencies.[68]

A byproduct of the deliberations of the Subcommittee on Chinese Revenue was the resolution adopted by the Conference regarding the reduction of Chinese military forces. A number of delegates, Robert Borden in particular, showed deep concern with the severe drain on the Chinese public revenue caused by the maintenance of large military forces. This concern afforded the main reason, if not exactly the pretext, for the unwillingness on the part of the powers to meet China's wishes for tariff autonomy and increased revenues. The idea of persuading China to reduce her military forces soon gained a firm hold on those participating in the Subcommittee and the full Committee. At the 22nd meeting of the Committee held on January 20, 1922, Borden, in support of the resolution, said that it was "inspired by a sincere and earnest desire to aid the purpose of the Chinese people in establishing a stable government and in freeing the country from the incubus of excessive militarism."[69] Solicitous about the current state of affairs, he added: "Up to the present there had been an unfortunate lack of such organizing capacity as would establish a strong and stable central government and bring the country once more under its effective direction and control. For such a purpose the provision of great revenues or the placing of large funds at the disposal of a weak administration was not of itself effective."[70] Then in a vein of guarded optimism, he concluded in these words: "But among all the tumult and the fluctuations attending the development of democracy in China, the attachment of the people to the soil and their untiring industry had remained unchanged. One might adapt the words of a well-known quotation: 'They hear the legions thunder past,/Then plunge in soil again.' Notwithstanding the present conditions, no one should fear for the future of the Chinese people."[71] Finally the Conference at the fifth plenary session on February 1, 1922,[72] formally approved the resolution by which an "earnest hope" was expressed that "immediate and effective steps may be taken by the Chinese government to reduce the aforesaid military force and expenditures." And this was done, according to the careful wording of the document, "without any intention to interfere in the internal problems of China." The Chinese delegation also gave its blessing to it because it was understood to have forestalled any movement to create a commission to make a general inquiry into the internal conditions in China.[73]

The Nine Power Treaty relating to the Chinese customs tariff was signed at Washington on February 6, 1922. It was to take effect on the date of the deposit of all the ratifications by the contracting powers. The revision of the tariff schedule to the limit of five per cent effective, which was not conditional on ratification, was duly begun and completed in that same year. In due time all powers except France ratified the treaty. (France delayed her ratification until 1925 when a dispute between her and China, known as the Gold Franc controversy, was settled to the satisfaction of France so that the Boxer Indemnity payments would be made in gold francs.)

Upon the coming into force of the treaty, the Special Conference[74] was, at China's invitation, held at Peking beginning on October 26, 1925, with thirteen powers attending, that is to say, with the four adhering powers of Denmark, Norway, Spain, and Sweden in addition to the original nine powers. Stress in the invitation was laid not only on the question of surtaxes but specifically on the right to exercise full tariff autonomy on the basis of Koo's declaration of January 5, 1922.

During the six months when the Special Tariff Conference was in session with the difficult and protracted discussions dragging on, the recurrent civil war flared up from time to time. At one time the capital where the Conference was seated was isolated and placed in a state of siege. Tuan Chi-jui, the Provisional Chief Executive, who opened the Conference, soon became a figurehead and was, in April 1926, finally deposed by the militarists. The Conference adjourned and was never resumed. That did not mean, however, that it had accomplished nothing. Two milestones were registered, though tentatively, on the road to the final goal of tariff autonomy: (1) In the draft article agreed to sometime in November, 1925, the contracting powers, recognizing China's right to tariff autonomy, agreed to remove the treaty restrictions on tariff, and gave consent to application of the Chinese National Tariff Law beginning January 1, 1929; (2) The table of proposed surtaxes which was submitted on March 25, 1926, by the American, British, and Japanese delegations as an amendment to a similar proposal made by China, divided all dutiable goods into seven classes and graded the rates of duty in such a manner that the new total rates would range from $7\frac{1}{2}$ to $27\frac{1}{2}$ per cent.

In the meantime Canton started to collect the $2\frac{1}{2}$ per cent surtaxes notwithstanding the protest of the treaty powers. In a few months this precedent was followed by all other Chinese ports. As a typical instance of realistic diplomacy, the British government in the course of the year 1926 more than once sought to legalize the *fait accompli* by urging the Powers to authorize the immediate and unconditional levy of the Washington surtaxes.

47

On July 25, 1928, representatives of the national government of China and the United States, namely, T. V. Soong, the Chinese Minister of Finance, and J. van A. MacMurray, the American Minister, signed in Peiping an agreement by which all treaty provisions between the two countries relating to tariff and related matters were annulled and tariff autonomy was restored to China, subject to the restrictions of the most favored nation clause. This lead was followed by all other powers. Japan was the last to align herself with the new policy. The first Chinese national tariff with rates of duty based in the main on the above-mentioned American-British-Japanese proposal of March 1926 was proclaimed and put into force on February 1, 1929. This important event in the history of Chinese diplomacy represented the first fissure in the structure of unequal treaties which had been built up in the course of almost a century. China thus realized one of the foremost aspects of the national sovereignty. The tree of tariff autonomy was planted at Washington; it began to blossom at Peking; it bore fruit at Peiping and Nanking.

Related Events

For a complete perspective on the Washington Conference, so far as the Chinese question was concerned, it is worthwhile to discuss briefly those related events which influenced the diplomacy on specific issues: (1) the Anglo-Japanese Alliance and the Lansing-Ishii agreement, (2) the Twenty-one Demands, (3) leased territories, and (4) extra-territoriality. Only the first of these questions was definitely disposed of at the Washington Conference, whereas the other three were partially or tentatively settled or not at all.

As was well known, the Anglo-Japanese Alliance was one of the most disquieting factors in the Far Eastern situation before the Conference was summoned. This alliance had aroused resentment in China, in the United States, and in some other countries. Even Great Britain was at times embarrassed by her commitments to Japan. One of the main purposes of the Conference was to find a possible solution for this dilemma. Collaterally with the work of the Conference, the Alliance was replaced by the Four Power Treaty of December 13, 1921 between the United States, the British Empire, France, and Japan. The signatories agreed to respect one another's insular possessions and dominions in the Pacific and to consider common measures for collective security in the event of a threatening situation. Still more unpopular was the Lansing-Ishii agreement of 1917, which embodied the doctrine that "territorial propinquity" created special relations between contiguous countries. It not only lapsed in consequence of the reinvigorated open door policy, but was formally cancelled by an exchange of notes between the American and Japanese governments in April, 1923.[75]

The presentation of the Twenty-one Demands by Japan in 1915 had aroused much hostility and indignation in China and in the United States. Adverse criticism in Japan itself was so severe that the event was considered by the wartime Foreign Minister of Japan, Mamoru Shigemitsu,[76] to be "a serious blunder that had an irretrievable effect on Japan's future path." Her international credit "fell disastrously" as a consequence of these negotiations. Again, Yamato Ichihashi, a Japanese author and a professor, had no hesitation in qualifying the demands with the adjectives "infamous" and "notorious" and Japan's diplomacy as "bullying."[77] Ichihashi's critical comments were specially significant inasmuch as his views were usually biased against China.

Unfortunately, the efforts made by China, first in Paris and then in Washington, to abrogate the resulting treaties and notes met with failure. During the debate on this subject, Shidehara at the 30th meeting of the Committee of the Whole on February 2, 1922, pointed out:

If it should once be recognized that rights solemnly granted by treaty may be revoked at any time on the ground that they were conceded against the spontaneous will of the grantor, an exceedingly dangerous precedent will be established, with far-reaching consequences upon the stability of the existing international relations in Asia, in Europe and everywhere.[78]

The following day the Chinese delegate, C. H. Wang, replied that

a still more dangerous precedent will be established with consequences upon the stability of international relations which cannot be estimated, if, without rebuke or protest from other Powers, one nation can obtain from a friendly, but in a military sense, weaker neighbour, and under circumstances such as attended the negotiation and signing of the treaties of 1915, valuable concessions which were not in satisfaction of pending controversies and for which no quid pro quo *was offered.*[79]

Arnold J. Toynbee thought that the argument advanced by the Chinese delegate had turned the tables effectively on his Japanese colleague.[80]

The result of the debate was most unsatisfactory. Would it have been better had the two parties agreed to undertake bilateral conversations on the Twenty-one Demands by adopting a procedure similar to that for the conduct of the Shantung conversations? This query must remain in the realm of conjecture. As it was, the net result was that Japan voluntarily made a few anticipated, matter-of-course concessions in China's favor. Japan agreed to withdraw the nefarious fifth group of demands, which were calculated to convert China into a Japanese protectorate. Japan also relinquished certain preferential rights which she could not have demanded without violating the open door principles. In regard to the Twenty-one Demands, the Conference did practically nothing to improve the existing situation. At the sixth plenary session, on February 4, 1922, the separate statements made by Japan, China, and the United States were merely recorded in the minutes. China reserved only the right to seek a solution of the entire question at some future negotiation. Japan's position in Manchuria was actually strengthened by the lack of Conference support for China's request that the treaties under review, in particular the South Manchurian treaty, be cancelled. Japan's position was so impregnable, said Root, that "it would be impossible to expel her unless by force."[81] Not until the Allied victory in 1945 was Japan expelled from Manchuria and the question of the Twenty-one Demands settled once and for all.

In the past there had been five foreign-leased territories in China: two in Shantung province, Kiaochow leased to Germany and Weihaiwei to Britain; two in Kwantung province, Kwangchow-wan leased to France and Kowloon to Britain; and the Kwangtung peninsula with Port Arthur and Dairen as the major ports, both of which were first leased to Russia and subsequently to Japan.

On December 3, 1921, at the 12th meeting of the Committee, Koo, in charge of this matter, presented China's case for the annulment and an early termination of these leases "in the interest not only of China, but of all nations, and especially with a view to the peace of the Far East."[82] As an outcome, Kiaochow and Weihaiwei were restored to China; Japan would not return her Manchurian leaseholds nor would Britain return the Kowloon extension; and France would only join in a collective restitution.

Today it is only the Kowloon area which remains in the hands of Great Britain, for the alleged reason that it is essential to the security of the port of Hongkong. Since the question is still pending, it seems useful to reproduce the words spoken by Koo in this connection:

As to the leased territory of Kowloon, leased to Great Britain, much is to be said for the importance of Hongkong to the trade of nations, and for the way in which its facilities are made accessible to the traders of the world, and while there may be a necessity to provide for the protection of the Hongkong Harbour in the interests of such trade, the retention of Kowloon may not necessarily be, in the view of the Chinese delegation, the sole solution of this problem.[83]

It was the extraterritoriality treaties which for one hundred years had restricted China's jurisdictional and administrative freedom of action toward aliens residing in her territory. This constituted the most flagrant impairment of her sovereign rights. At the turn of the century, the big powers began to show some inclination toward relinquishment of their special rights, but only on condition that they were satisfied with the state of the Chinese laws and with arrangements for their administration.

When the question was brought before the Conference, C. H. Wang, in his statement at the sixth meeting of the Committee held on November 25, 1921,[84] asked the powers to agree on a definite period at the end of which extraterritorial rights would be surrendered. The Conference adopted a resolution by which a future commission was to be established in China to inquire into the actual practice of consular jurisdiction as well as into the laws, judicial system and administration of China, and then to make a report with recommendations. In January 1926 the commission of inquiry was formed in Peking collaterally with the Tariff Conference. The commission had as members representatives of those powers which took part in the Tariff Conference. Almost a year was spent in on-the-spot investigations of the courts, prisons, and other related matters in a number of ports and cities in China. A report was drawn up setting forth a series of recommendations, according to which the abolition of extraterritoriality must, as said before, go through the slow process of careful preparation over an indefinite period of time. The report was shelved. Neither did the separate negotiations conducted by China in the late 1920's with a number of European powers produce anything concrete. The powers were only prepared to join in a more or less collective surrender of extraterritorial rights. China once made an attempt to terminate the unequal treaties unilaterally, but that attempt, too, proved abortive.

During the second phase of World War II, when China

became an ally of the United States, the United Kingdom, and others, the two English-speaking powers took the initiative in negotiating with China new treaties on the basis of equality and reciprocity. These are the treaties of Chungking and Washington, of the same date, January 11, 1943, between China and the United Kingdom and between China and the United States. The happy example was soon followed by all other powers. By these new treaties, extra-territoriality and all other anomalous conditions were brought to an end without further delay. The century-old system thus faded into past history. A new era of international relations had been inaugurated in China.

Evaluating the Conference

As an outcome of the Washington Conference, China scored two major successes: *first*, the disposal of the Shantung controversy; and, *second*, the laying of firm foundations for the attainment of tariff autonomy. She was less fortunate in all other matters. The general feeling on the part of the participating powers then was that before China could hope to have her aspirations realized, she must first put her own house in order and be in a position to present at least a semblance of stable government.

While the original idea underlying the four principles of Elihu Root was to provide the fullest and most unembarrassed opportunity to China to develop and maintain for herself an effective and stable government, China failed to avail herself of it, nor was such an opportunity actually given her. What was worse was that the pious assurances contained in those principles, coupled with and reinforced by the naval treaty, tended to lull China and the other powers alike into a false sense of security. By subsequently embarking on a chain of aggressions against China, Japan proceeded to create an extremely embarrassing and confusing situation for China and to place serious obstacles in the path of China's national reconstruction. Not only that, but Japan must have made full use of the intermission in the post-Conference years to prepare her plans of aggression. So far as Japan was concerned, she must have regarded the second decade of the century as a sort of *entr'acte* in the long Japanese play of conquest and domination. Indeed, a collection of nice words incorporated in an international instrument—respect for integrity and independence, for non-aggression, for peaceful coexistence, for non-interference in internal affairs, and the like—more often than not serves as a smoke screen behind which prospective aggressors act in exactly opposite directions. Such an instrument offers at best a temporary respite and not a real protection to the intended victims.

Purely from the historical point of view, with all ethical and juridical considerations brushed aside for the time being, it appears that whenever aggression occurs, it is not altogether correct to lay the blame wholly at the aggressor's door. It goes without saying that the aggressor must bear the principal responsibility, but the victim and the bystanders, too, share the blame. It is usually the weakness of the victim, in the military, political, or economic sense, aggravated by the inadequacy of support from others, that invites and encourages aggression. In the international domain, lack of individual or collective strength invariably constitutes a source of danger. To cite a Chinese literary saying: When something becomes rotten worms will eat into it.

物必自腐也而後蟲生之.

Recognizing the responsibility of the victim by no means sanctions aggression. The fact that a person has not properly locked the door at night, or that a bank teller helplessly watches piles of banknotes being snatched away at the pistol's point, does not absolve the bandit from his crime, nor does it make the criminal act less so. What is correct in the relationship between man and man should, in this regard, be also correct in the relationship between state and state. In the international arena, while from time to time a number of unpleasant facts and situations have to be faced, the soundness of certain fundamental principles which govern or ought to govern the conduct of international relations should never be questioned. One such principle is that of peace with justice as exemplified in the Covenant of the League of Nations and in the Charter of the United Nations. Nothing is more abhorrent and more likely to lead to war than the settlement of international problems based upon appeasement and expediency. A gap always exists between theories and realities. It is the never-ending task of a statesman to bridge it as much as possible. As history shows, the well-founded rules of conduct of a civilized community sink into obscurity when the international situation worsens steadily or when a world war breaks out but rise again to renewed heights when the situation improves or when the war ends. In the meantime, the significant fact remains, it should be repeated with emphasis, that it is only through unity and strength, individual as well as collective, that serious international crises can be coped with, principles can be made to apply to facts, and right can be expected to prevail over might.

Bethesda, Maryland
January 1, 1963.

NOTES

[1] For details, see Westel W. Willoughby's *China at the Conference: A Report* (hereinafter called *Report*), (Baltimore, the Johns Hopkins Press, 1922). See also the article written by Stanley K. Hornbeck, "Principles and Policies in regard to China," *Foreign Affairs*, Vol. I, No. 2, (December 15, 1922), pp. 120-135,—a paper in which the writer ably analyzed the proceedings of the Conference and ended up with a note of cautious optimism.

[2] See Note No. 40.

[3] This and the following passages were quoted from President Harding's two addresses, *Foreign Relations of the United States*, 1922, Vol. I, pp. 310, 377.

[4] This chapter is in fact a continuation of the article previously written by the same author, entitled "Woodrow Wilson, Wellington Koo and the China Question at the Paris Peace Conference," printed by A. W. Sythoff, Leyden, 1959. This article, with slight revisions, was subsequently reprinted at the request of Dr. Paul K. T. Sih, director of the Institute of Asian Studies, St. John's University, New York. Its new title is "China at the Paris Peace Conference, 1919" printed by St. John's University Press, Jamaica, New York, 1961.

[5] London *Times*, August 6, 1919.

[6] Telegram from Hughes to American Legation in Peking and American Embassy in Tokyo, September 19, 1921, *Foreign Relations*, 1921, Vol. I, p. 621. "It is necessary," Hughes said in conclusion, "constantly to bear in mind, however, that the United States cannot place itself, in any

phase of the negotiations, in the position of either acting or appearing to act as an attorney for either China or Japan."

[7] Telegram from the U.S. Chargé d'affaires in Japan (Bell) to Hughes, July 26, 1921, transmitting a memorandum of the same date from the Japanese Foreign Office. *Foreign Relations*, 1921, Vol. I, p. 45.

[8] *For. Rel., ibid.,* p. 58

[9] *The Chinese Delegation to the Washington Conference: Conversations between the Chinese and the Japanese Representatives in regard to the Shantung Question,* 1923, Washington Government Printing Office, pp. 3 & 4.

[10] *Senate Document* (hereinafter called *Sen. Doc.*), 67th Congress, 2nd Session, 1921-22, Vol. 10, p. 526.

[11] Quotations taken from the publication entitled *Conversations between the Chinese and Japanese Representatives in regard to the Shantung Question: Minutes of the Proceedings prepared by the Japanese Delegation and printed by the U.S. Government Printing Office at Washington,* 1923 (hereinafter called *Minutes*). For this quotation, see p. 12. Particulars will be given only in the case of direct quotations.

[12] Here the author ventures to reproduce a letter which he, serving as junior secretary of the Chinese delegation at Paris in 1919, addressed to his immediate superior, Dr. Koo, dated June 16, 1919. It reads:

"I wish to invite your attention to the passages in the summary of the German Counter-proposals and the Allied Reply of to-day's date, relating to Shantung and Kiaochow.

"The German counter-proposal reads to the substantial effect that Germany accepts the Shantung-Kiaochow deci-

sion, but expects to be compensated for the properties owned by the Germans. Please see, also, to-day's "La Libre Parole" and to-night's "Le Temps."

"The Allied reply says that all movable and immovable properties in a ceded territory will be ceded to the Power in whose favor the territorial cession is to be made, but that the principles of private property will apply to the case of Kiaochow, if the Germans can establish the private ownership of the railway and mines owned by them.

"It is, therefore, most likely that the Japanese have to buy the railway and mines from the Germans. Will it be practicable for us to make an attempt to repurchase the same from the Japanese? If so, is it not advisable to intimate the idea beforehand to the Council of the Chiefs of State?"

signed: Wunsz King

[13] 14th meeting, December 16, 1921, *Minutes,* p. 122.

[14] 15th meeting, December 17, 1921, *Ibid.,* p. 139.

[15] Telegram dated Peking, No. 106, December 31, 1921, *Waichiaopu Archives* through the courtesy of the Institute of Modern History, Academia Sinica, Taipei.

Liang's biographers explained that it was a matter of protocol for Obata to come to extend congratulations to the new Premier upon his assumption of premiership, and that the purpose of the visit was not to conduct negotiations. As regards the question of a loan, they went on to say, the best thing to be hoped for would be one to be arranged by the Chinese people themselves, or else it should be arranged through the joint efforts of both domestic and foreign financiers. Nothing had been said to suggest that the source of the loan should be limited to the Japanese or that Japan should be given priority in this matter. *Biography of San Sui S. Y. Liang* (in Chinese), compiled by a number of Liang's former students in Kwantung Province and printed in Hongkong, December 1939, Vol. 2, p. 184.

Said a circular telegram issued in the name of the entire Cabinet in Peking, January 12, 1922: When Obata came to offer congratulations on December 28 (29?), and spoke about the question of the Kiaochow-Tsinan railway, the only reply given by the Premier was that our policy was to provide funds for its redemption under our own management, and that this should be settled by our delegates at the Washington Conference. The Premier also made it clear that the interview was a personal conversation, and that an official reply must be made by the Ministry of Foreign Affairs. Neither the Cabinet nor the Ministry had any subsequent contact with Obata in regard to this matter. *Ibid.,* Vol. 2, p. 190.

[16] Telegram Peking, No. 107, *Waichiaopu Archives op. cit.*

[17] The gist of this interview was subsequently communicated to the Chinese delegation by MacMurray at the request of Hughes. Koo has confirmed this in his letter to the author, dated June 25, 1961.

[18] See his dispatch to the American Minister in Peking, Schurman, February 15, 1922, *For. Rel.,* 1922, Vol. I, p. 962.

[19] Koo's letter to King, January 7, 1961.

[20] Dr. T. L. Yuan's article "Huang Fu's part in the Washington Conference: A Retrospect," *Collection of Essays* (in Chinese), *in Memory of the late Huang Fu* (1879-1936), p. 116. Huang Fu (then Lieutenant General) was an adviser to the delegation. An author and a statesman, he was the chief civil authority in North China when the Tangku Armistice Agreement was concluded with the Japanese military authorities on May 31, 1933.

[21] While no record of the Liang-Obata interview can be

found today, that of the Yen-Obata interview is kept in the *Waichiaopu Archives op. cit.* Mr. K. K. Kwok was so kind as to send the author a copy of the same together with that of a telegram addressed by the Waichiaopu to the delegates reporting a gist of the interview, December 28, 1921, Peking No. 103. He had obtained copies of these papers from the Institute of Modern History of Academia Sinica.

[22] Schurman's telegram to Hughes, January 15, 1922, *For. Rel.*, 1922, Vol. I, p. 682.

[23] Telegram from the Chinese delegates to Waichiaopu, January 4, 1922, *Waichiaopu Archives op. cit.*

[24] Schurman's telegrams to Hughes, January 15 & 16, 1922, *For. Rel.*, 1922, Vol. I, pp. 682 & 940; cf. Liang's *Biography,* Vol. 2, p. 191.

[25] Liang's *Biography,* Vol. 2, pp. 188-190.

[26] Schurman's telegram to Hughes, February 4, 1922, *For. Rel.*, 1922, Vol. I, p. 686.

[27] Shidehara spoke about the interview between the Chinese Minister of Foreign Affairs and the Japanese Minister but he was obviously referring in particular to the Liang-Obata interview. See 18th meeting, Jan. 4, 1922, *Minutes,* p. 175.

[28] 20th meeting, January 6, 1922, *Minutes,* p. 199.

[29] MacMurray's letter to the author, Captiva, Florida, November 13, 1958.

[30] Summaries of the three interviews with the two delegations separately as well as the one with the Chinese delegates on January 30, 1922, were quoted from the annexes

to the State Department Document File No. 793.94/1300a, being a letter from Hughes to Schurman, dated February 15, 1922. Consultation of this paper was made possible through the courtesy of the National Archives and Records Service, Washington, D.C. Cf. *For. Rel.*, 1922, Vol. I, p. 963.

[31] Hughes to Schurman, January 22, 1922, *For. Rel.*, 1922, Vol. I, p. 942.

The formula also contained a provision by which the Chinese Government might appoint an assistant traffic manager of Chinese nationality after two and a half years from the date of the transfer of the railway. This provision was agreed to by the two delegations and recorded in the agreed minutes. In this connection it should be recalled that at the 16th meeting, December 19, 1921, Shidehara said that the Japanese delegation would feel satisfied with the post of a Japanese assistant or district traffic manager who would be responsible for the Shantung branch only, while there should be a Chinese general traffic manager for the combined system of the Tientsin-Pukow and Tsingtao-Tsinan lines (*Minutes*, pp. 151, 153-4). The Chinese delegation turned down this suggestion on account of the strong opposition of the "Chinese people here" (meaning the "People's delegates" and the delegate of Shantung province and others). Shidehara, however, made another suggestion that China would appoint her own manager and also a Japanese expert as an associate manager; this was not accepted either (*Ibid.*, p. 160). Cf. Note. No. 21: During the Yen-Obata interview, the latter said that the employment of Japanese as assistant officials was Shidehara's personal idea only.

[32] *For. Rel.*, 1922, Vol. I, pp. 941-3.

[33] Hughes to Schurman, January 25, 1922, *Ibid.*, p. 945.

[34] Hughes to Schurman, February 15, 1922, *Ibid.*, p. 964.

[35] H. H. Ling's *A Comprehensive Survey of Railway Development in China* (in Chinese), published in Taiwan, July 1954, p. 196.

[36] Information supplied through the courtesy of the Chinese Ministry of Communications, Taipei.

[37] Cf. a telegram from Schurman to Hughes, December 3, 1921, *For. Rel.*, 1921, Vol. I, pp. 315-321, presenting a full and frank survey of the internal situation then obtaining in China.

[38] Certain payments on the Chicago Continental Bank loan.

[39] *For. Rel.*, 1922, Vol. I, pp. 271-2.

[40] *Sen. Doc.*, pp. 443-5. Text of the ten points as follows:
In conformity with the agenda of the Conference, the Chinese Government proposes for the consideration of and adoption by the Conference the following general principles to be applied in the determination of the questions relating to China:

1. (a) The Powers engage to respect and observe the territorial integrity and political and administrative independence of the Chinese Republic.

(b) China upon her part is prepared to give an undertaking not to alienate or lease any portion of her territory or littoral to any Power.

2. China, being in full accord with the principle of the so-called open door or equal opportunity for the commerce and industry of all nations having treaty relations with China, is prepared to accept and apply it in all parts of the Chinese Republic without exception.

3. With a view to strengthening mutual confidence and maintaining peace in the Pacific and the Far East the Powers agree not to conclude between themselves any treaty

or agreement directly affecting China or the general peace in these regions without previously notifying China and giving to her an opportunity to participate.

4. All special rights, privileges, immunities or commitments, whatever their character or contractual basis, claimed by any of the Powers in or relating to China are to be declared, and all such or future claims not so made known are to be deemed null and void. The rights, privileges, immunities and commitments, not known or to be declared are to be examined with a view to determining their scope and validity and, if valid, to harmonizing them with one another and with the principles declared by this Conference.

5. Immediately or as soon as circumstances will permit, existing limitations upon China's political jurisdictional and administrative freedom of action are to be removed.

6. Reasonable, definite terms of duration are to be attached to China's present commitments which are without time limits.

7. In the interpretation of instruments granting special rights or privileges, the well-established principle of construction that such grants shall be strictly construed in favor of the grantors, is to be observed.

8. China's rights as a neutral are to be fully respected in future wars to which she is not a party.

9. Provision is to be made for the peaceful settlement of international disputes in the Pacific and the Far East.

10. Provision is to be made for conferences to be held from time to time for the discussion of international questions relative to the Pacific and Far East, as a basis for the determination of common policies of the Signatory Powers in relation thereto.

[41] *Sen. Doc.*, pp. 450-1.

[42] *Ibid.*, pp. 448, 451-2, and 454.

[43] See below, chapter on Chinese customs tariff questions.

[44] *Sen. Doc.*, pp. 454-460.

[45] Willoughby, *Report*, pp. 194-6; Arnold J. Toynbee *Survey of International Affairs*, 1920-23, (Oxford University Press, London, 1925), pp. 448-452.

[46] Willoughby, *op. cit.*, p. 197, fn.2.

[47] *Ibid.*, p. 43.

[48] *For. Rel.*, 1922, Vol. I, p. 279, footnote 60.

[49] See Dr. T. L. Yuan's article *op. cit., Collection of Essays,* etc., (note 20), pp. 115-116.

[50] Telegrams between Hughes and Schurman, December 7 & 11, 1921, *For. Rel.*, 1922, Vol. I, pp. 275-6.

[51] Dr. Yuan's article *op. cit.*

[52] The nineteen participating Powers: Australia, Belgium, Bolivia, Canada, China, Denmark, France, Great Britain, India, Italy, Mexico, New Zealand, The Netherlands, Norway, Portugal, Sweden, the Union of South Africa, the United States and the U.S.S.R. Germany declined the invitation to take part.

[53] *For. Rel.*, 1921, Vol. I, p. 79.

[54] *Ibid.*, p. 82.

[55] *Sen. Doc.*, pp. 469-471.

[56] See *antea*, Note No. 43.

[57] *Conference on the Limitation of Armament: Subcommittees* (hereinafter called *Subcommittees*), Washington, November 12, 1921–February 6, 1922, (Washington, Government Printing Office, 1922), p. 546.

[58] A provincial transit duty in China on commodities which was originally levied to meet the expenditures of the military campaigns against the Taiping rebels in the middle of the 19th century. It was finally abolished in 1929.

[59] Treaties of 1843 and 1844 between China and Great Britain, and America, and France, and subsequently with other countries.

[60] *Subcommittees,* p. 558.

[61] This account was compiled by the author entirely from his memory. The notes he had prepared in both English and Chinese while attending the meetings of the Subcommittee are no longer available today. Cf. *Ibid.*, pp. 560-568.

[62] 4th meeting of the Subcommittee, December 28, 1921, *Ibid.*, p. 588.

[63] *Ibid.*, p. 590.

[64] *Ibid.*, p. 592.

[65] This episode happened during the 6th meeting of the Subcommittee on Drafting held on January 14, 1922. The account here was based on the author's own notes: cf. *Subcommittees*, p. 472, in which the whole story was covered by the two words "after discussion."

[66] *Sen. Doc.,* pp. 594-597.

[67] *Ibid.*, p. 598.

[68] Willoughby, *Report,* pp. 92-94, but Underwood's views in this regard were not recorded in the official minutes, cf. *Sen. Doc.,* pp. 607-8.

[69] *Sen. Doc.,* p. 655.

[70] *Ibid.,* p. 656.

[71] *Ibid.,* p. 657.

[72] *Ibid.,* pp. 120-121.

[73] Willoughby, *Report,* p. 110, footnote.

[74] For details concerning the proceedings of the Peking Tariff Conference of 1925-1926 and the aftermath, etc., consult Stanley F. Wright's *China's Struggle for Tariff Autonomy,* (Shanghai, Kelly & Walsh, 1938), pp. 461-691.

[75] Toynbee, *Survey* etc. *op. cit.,* p. 470.

[76] *Japan and Her Destiny,* written in Japanese by Mamoru Shigemitsu and translated into English by Oswald White, (Dutton, New York, 1958), pp. 39, 40.

[77] *The Washington Conference and After,* (Stanford University Press, California, 1928), pp. 191, 289.

[78] *Sen. Doc.,* p. 754.

[79] *Ibid.,* p. 777.

[80] *Survey op. cit.,* p. 470, footnote.

[81] Koo's interview with Elihu Root, December 15, 1921, at the Navy Building, Washington, D.C.

[82] *Sen. Doc.*, p. 540.

[83] 13th meeting of the Committee, December 7, 1921, *Ibid.*, p. 552.

[84] *Ibid.*, p. 477.

Appendix: Dr. Koo's statement
regarding the re-establishment of tariff autonomy, cf. p. 44.

On November 23 last, I had the honor, on behalf of the Chinese Delegation, to lay the Tariff question of China before the Committee. Three propositions were submitted. The principal one of them was for the restoration to China of her Tariff Autonomy, the other two being intended merely as provisional measures to prepare the ground for the early consummation of the main object. At the same time I stated that it was not the intention of the Chinese Government to effect any change that might disturb the present administration of the Chinese Maritime Customs, though this statement obviously could not be reasonably construed to preclude China's legitimate aspirations gradually to make this important branch of the Chinese Government more national in character.

I explained the reasons why China was desirous of recovering her freedom of action in respect to the matter of levying Customs duties. The Committee, after some discussion, referred the whole question to a Sub-Committee, of which Senator Underwood has been the distinguished Chairman. The results of the discussions in the Sub-Committee are embodied in an agreement which has just been laid before you. It is a valuable agreement, embodying, as it does, a number of important points, connected with the effective application of the present regime of Treaty Tariff. But it will be noted that the question of the restoration of Tariff Autonomy to China is not included, it being the opinion of some members of the Sub-Committee that it would not be practicable to fix at present a definite period within which the existing Treaty provisions on Tariff were to be brought to an end, and that the question should be decided in the light of conditions that might arise in the future.

The Chinese delegation, however, cannot but wish that a different view had prevailed. Tariff Autonomy is a sovereign right enjoyed by all independent states. Its free exercise is essential to the well-being of the state. The existing Treaty provisions, by which the levy of Customs duties, transit dues, and other imposts is regulated, constitute not only a restriction on China's freedom of action, but an infringement on her sovereignty. Restoration to her of Tariff Autonomy would only be recognition of a right which is hers, and which she has relinquished against her will.

The maintenance of the present Tariff *regime* means, moreover, a continued loss of revenue to the Chinese Government. The Customs import duty under this *regime* is limited to the very low rate of 5 per cent *ad valorem* for all classes of dutiable goods, compared with the average rate of 15 per cent to 60 per cent levied by other countries. In fact, because the duties are levied on the basis of a previously fixed schedule, the actual collections amount to only 3½ per cent effective. The Customs revenue, therefore, constitutes only about 7½ per cent of China's total revenue, while the average for the principal countries in the West ranges from 12 per cent to 15 per cent at present, and still higher before the war. When the proposed surtax of 2½ per cent for ordinary articles and of 5 per cent on certain luxuries eventually goes into effect, more revenue will be produced, but even then it will hardly be commensurate with the rapidly growing needs of the Chinese Government. Much of the elasticity of the fiscal systems of other States depends upon their freedom to regulate their Customs duties. To provide the fullest and most unembarrassed opportunity to China to develop and maintain for herself an effective and stable Government, it is necessary to restore Tariff Autonomy to her at an early date.

The necessity to levy a uniform low duty has encouraged

a disproportionate increase in the import of luxuries such as wine and tobacco; and apart from the loss of revenue consequent upon giving these things the same rate as is levied on the necessaries of life, the effect on the social and moral habits of the Chinese people has been altogether deleterious. A beginning has been made in the agreement before the Committee in authorizing a levy of an additional surtax of 2½ per cent on certain articles of luxury, but it is apparent that a greater increase is needed if a restraining influence is to be exercised in the use of these articles of luxury.

Nor is it to be overlooked that the present Treaty Tariff *regime* is an impediment to China's economic development. Under this *regime* China enjoys no reciprocity from any of the Powers with which she stands in treaty relations. Though every •Treaty Power enjoys the advantage of having its wares imported into China at the exceptionally low rate of 5 per cent *ad valorem,* Chinese produce and merchandise, on entering into any of these countries, is subjected to the maximum rates leviable, which are in some cases 60 or 70 times the rate which she herself levies on foreign imports. The necessity of levying uniform duties on all articles imported into China, on the other hand, makes these duties on such articles as machinery and raw materials for Chinese industries a handicap to China's industrial development. At present there are more than 1,000 Chinese factories employing foreign machinery and methods and engaged in over 30 different kinds of important industries. To enable them to live and develop and thereby contribute to the growth of China's foreign trade in which all nations are deeply interested, some latitude is necessary in the regulation of the Customs duties.

Besides, regulation of China's Tariff by Treaty must inevitably, in the nature of things, work unjustly and to her great detriment. Thus, whenever China makes a proposal, be it for revision of the Tariff to bring it more into harmony with the prevailing prices or for an increase of the Customs duty to meet her increased needs, the unanimous consent of more than a dozen Treaty Powers is necessary. As each country naturally desires to protect and promote its own commercial interests in China, and as the industries of the Treaty Powers vary in character and they export different kinds of merchandise, they all seek to avoid the burden of the new revision or increased rate falling upon the industries of their own countries. With this end in view, different conditions are not infrequently attached by different Powers to their consent to revise the Customs Tariff or increase the rate.

Thus, though this matter of Customs Tariff is intimately connected with the well-being of the Chinese State, the interests of the Treaty Powers appear to be placed at times before the legitimate interests of China. Under such circumstances the difficulty of effecting any adjustment or arrangement favourable to China can easily be conceived, and it has at times been well-nigh insurmountable. On one occasion or another there is always some Power who considers its own interest in the matter of the Chinese Customs Tariff more important than the supreme interests of China. The experience of the Chinese delegation in the Sub-Committee on Tariff, much as it has accomplished, has not altogether removed the ground for this opinion. But as unanimity is required, the dissent of one Power is sufficient to defeat and upset a general arrangement agreed to by all the others, while by virtue of the most favoured nation clause, a concession or privilege granted by China to one nation for a specific consideration is at once claimed by all without regard to the *quid pro quo*.

In view of the inherent difficulty and injustice of the present *regime*, and of the wholesome and desirable effect which restoration of Tariff Autonomy is sure to have upon the trade and economic development of China, as well as upon the evolution of her fiscal system, the Chinese Delegation feel in duty bound to declare that though this Committee does not see its way to consider China's claim for the restoration of her Tariff Autonomy, it is not their desire, in assenting to the agreement now before you, to relinquish their claim; on the contrary, it is their intention to bring the question up again for consideration on all appropriate occasions in the future.

CHINA
and the Nine Power Conference at Brussels in
1937

Tsien Tai

CHINA
and the Nine Power Conference at Brussels in
1937

Tsien Tai

St. John's University Press, New York
1964

Published under the auspices of the
Institute of Asian Studies, St. John's University

© Copyright 1964 by St. John's University, New York

Also in this series

NO. 1
THE CHINESE REVOLUTION OF 1911
by Chin-Tung Liang

NO. 2
CHINA AT THE PARIS PEACE CONFERENCE IN 1919
by Wunsz King

NO. 3
CHINA AT THE WASHINGTON CONFERENCE, 1921-22
by Wunsz King

PREFACE

The Nine Power Conference at Brussels in 1937 was important in China's contemporary political development for two major reasons:

1. The Conference provided the best hope for a peaceful settlement, since the League of Nations had failed to deal with the Sino-Japanese dispute.

2. The Conference would give an acid-test to the validity of the Nine Power Treaty of Washington, 1922, safeguarding the sovereignty, the independence, and the territorial and administrative integrity of China.

The Conference failed to achieve these objectives. Japan boycotted the Conference. Germany, though invited, refused to attend. Italy, although she participated in the Conference, was in favor of Japan's aggressive position. However, in spite of these difficulties, the Conference did have some positive achievements.

These are found in the resolutions taken by the Conference. Though falling short of concrete action, these resolutions did set a basic moral concept in proper perspective: Japan was the aggressor and China the victim. This ideological commitment proved to be of vital importance to the later development of the Western alliance against the totalitarian front of Nazi Germany, Fascist Italy, and Imperialist Japan during World War II.

Dr. Tsien Tai, author of this monograph, had been a delegate of China to the League of Nations. When the Conference took place at Brussels, Dr. Tai was Chinese Ambassador to Belgium and participated in the Conference as one of China's delegates. I personally had an intimate working experience with him, because during the Conference I was stationed in Italy on a special diplomatic mission relating to this very meeting at Brussels. Dr. Tsien's lucid account, based upon personal experience and original source materials, provides new thought for students interested in Far Eastern affairs.

We list this study as No. 4 of the "Asia in the Modern World Series," as it is closely related to the previous issue of this series, *China at the Washington Conference, 1921-1922*, which deals with the Nine Power Treaty.

In publishing this work we wish to pay our tribute to the author, an eminent Chinese scholar and diplomat, who passed away from a heart ailment on July 31, 1962, in New York. May this study of his remain as a lasting memory for all those who knew, loved, and respected him.

Paul K. T. Sih, *Director*
Institute of Asian Studies
St. John's University
New York

CHINA and the NINE POWER CONFERENCE at BRUSSELS in 1937

The Origin of the Brussels Conference

On the night of July 7, 1937, Japan deliberately attacked China at Lukouchiao, or the Marco Polo bridge, about nine miles southwest of Peiping. On July 16, the Chinese government dispatched a memorandum to the signatories of the Nine Power Treaty, pointing out that "the sudden attack on Lukouchiao and the invasion of North China by large Japanese military forces constitute a clear violation of China's sovereignty, contrary to the letter and spirit of the Nine Power Treaty, the Paris Peace Pact, and the Covenant of the League of Nations."

On August 13, the second battle of Shanghai began. On September 12, Dr. V. K. Wellington Koo, Chinese Ambassador in Paris and Representative on the Council of the League of Nations, presented to the Secretary General of the League of Nations an appeal from the Chinese government under articles 10, 11, and 17 of the Covenant. On September 15, Dr. Koo addressed the 18th Assembly, which subsequently turned the matter over to its Far Eastern Advisory Committee. This was deemed a wise maneuver for two reasons: first, although the United States was not a member of the League, it was represented on the Advisory Committee as a non-voting member and as such would be able to bring its world influence to bear on the dispute; and secondly, the Assembly could for a time shelve its responsibility to apply sanctions against Japan under the provisions of the League Covenant, a step which had proved impractical in the Italian-Abyssinian war experience. On October 5, the Advisory Committee adopted two reports: the first report denounced Japan as the treaty violator; the second report suggested that the League should invite "those members of the League who were parties to the Nine Power Treaty to initiate at the earliest possible moment the consultation and full and frank communication provided for by that treaty." It further suggested that other states possessing special interests in the Far East should, if possible, be associated with this work. Koo accepted the suggestion with a reservation "to present the matter before the Council on future appropriate occasions." On October 6, the Assembly finally adopted the committee's reports and resolution. Thereafter, the United States signified her general accord with the decision of the Assembly of the League of Nations.

The idea of the Nine Power Treaty Conference came from the British delegation. It was warmly supported by the other members because they thought (a) it would involve the United States in more active participation to solve the dispute; (b) the question of sanctions could thus be avoided; (c) Japan, which was no longer a member of the League and would not attend a meeting of the League, might be willing to attend the Nine Power Treaty Conference, since she was still a party to that treaty.

Following the Assembly's adoption of the committee's second report, the President of the Assembly addressed letters to those members of the League which were parties to the Nine Power Treaty. At the same time, the United Kingdom conferred with the United States for the purpose of convening the Nine Power Conference.

In spite of the concurrence of the British and American governments, neither country wanted to be the inviting power because American public opinion was not yet ripe, and as the success of the conference was doubtful from the beginning, London and Washington would be much embarrassed in case of failure. France and Holland were the next possible inviting powers, but both of them were reluctant in view of the inadequacy of their defense power in

2

the Far East and their consequent desire not to offend Japan. Finally, the British government, with the approval of the government of the United States, requested the Belgian government to be the host of the conference. The Belgian government, after some hesitation, accepted the request. On October 16, invitations were sent to the signatories of the Nine Power Treaty, proposing that they should meet at Brussels on October 30. The date was later postponed to November 3.

The Belgian Invitation and the Participating Powers

The Belgian invitation was sent to all the other signatories of the Nine Power Treaty, namely, the original signatories (China, Great Britain, the U.S.A., France, Italy, Japan, the Netherlands, and Portugal) plus the adhering powers (Bolivia, Sweden, Denmark, Norway, and Mexico). All accepted with the exception of Japan. In her reply of October 27, Japan claimed that her action was a measure of self-defense and did not violate the Nine Power Treaty. She also pointed out that the conference had connections with the League, whose resolutions were unfriendly to Japan.

Since the League's resolution suggested that "other states possessing special interests in the Far East be associated with this work," the Belgian government, acting in accord with the accepting powers, extended invitations to Germany and the U.S.S.R. The Soviet government accepted, while Germany declined on the ground that she was not a party of the treaty. However, she offered her co-operation "in any effort towards a peaceful settlement of the conflict when the indispensable conditions for a friendly adjustment were present."

In fact, Germany, as an ally of Japan under the anti-Comintern agreement of November 25, 1936, did not want to offend Japan. On the other hand, she was at that time on friendly relations with China and wished to avoid an embarrassing position.

Thus the number of actual participants of the Conference was nineteen, namely: Australia, Belgium, Bolivia, Canada, China, Denmark, France, Great Britain, India, Italy, Mexico, Norway, New Zealand, the Netherlands, Portugal, Sweden, the Union of South Africa, the United States, and the Soviet Union.

The Formal Opening of the Conference

At the opening meeting of the conference on November 3, Mr. Spaak, the Belgian foreign minister, regretted the absence of Japan and Germany and expressed the hope that Germany's attitude might be modified when the indispensable conditions were present. The statements of Norman Davis (U.S.A.), Anthony Eden (U.K.), and Yvon Delbos (France) all expressed devotion to the sanctity of treaties and hope that the conference would succeed in bringing about a fair and just settlement. Only Italy, as a member of the tripartite Anti-Comintern Pact, asserted that unless the realities of the situation were taken into account, nothing would result from the meeting and that the only thing the conference could do was to bring the two parties into direct negotiations. It was exactly what Japan would have said. In a vigorous speech, Dr. Koo said:

For four months the weight of Japan's mighty war machine has been brought to bear upon innocent, peace-loving China by land, sea, and air. . . . Japanese military occupation of North China covers practically three whole provinces, Hopeh, Chahar, and Sui-yuan. They have also occupied parts of the provinces of Shantung and Shansi. They have entered Chapei and Kiangwan in Shanghai, which the Chinese forces evacuated after gallantly holding out for seventy-seven days against the most formidable attacks of Japan's modern mechanized forces. Five Japanese armies totaling more than half a million men continue to attack the Chinese defense lines on five fronts with a view to forcing a rapid victory in order to impress and to overawe the conference. . . .

4

In the light of the history of the past few years in the Far East, it is evident that the present outbreak of Japanese armed aggression is merely a continuation of Japan's policy of territorial expansion on the Asiatic mainland, already betrayed in all its flagrancy at the time of her attack on Mukden in 1931 with her subsequent military occupation of Manchuria and Jehol.

The setting up of a puppet regime in Manchuria propped up by the Kwantung army and packed with Japanese advisers in all key posts has been only a camouflage for territorial conquest. The invasion of Chinese provinces inside the Great Wall; the occupation of Eastern Chahar in 1933; Japan's peremptory demand in 1935 for removal of the governor and other high officials of Hopeh, for the evacuation of the central government troops therefrom, and for the expulsion of the Kuomingtang party workers from the same area; her creation in December of the same year of the so-called East Hopeh autonomous and anti-communist regime with the aid and protection of the Japanese military guards; her military occupation of north Chahar; and the open attempts of the Japanese military agents in the past two years to establish an autonomous government for the five provinces of North China—all these acts and activities in contravention of international law and Japan's own treaty obligations show only too clearly her sinister design on China, with whom she claims to have been at peace.

We desire peace but we know that we cannot obtain it in the presence of Japanese aggression. It is not a peace at any price that will either render justice to China or do credit to civilization. It is only by accepting a peace based upon the principles of the Nine Power Treaty that China, by her tremendous sacrifices during the past few months, will be contributing to the cause of law and order in the relations between nations.

At the conference there were several currents of opinion. The first group was represented by the great majority of powers, including the United Kingdom, the United States, and France. They insisted that the aim of the conference was "to consider friendly methods for expediting the end of the regrettable conflict," as the Belgian government had put it in its letter of invitation. They did not want to do anything further than mediation. If conciliation failed, they had no other plans.

The second group believed that, in case conciliation failed, some positive step to help China should be adopted. This group consisted of the Soviet Union, Mexico, and New Zealand. But because various powers were afraid that Japan might be offended if they sided too closely with the Soviet Union, when the question of forming a subcommittee was discussed, they at first wanted to exclude the Soviet Union. Litvinov was disgusted and left Brussels on November 9. After that, nothing more was heard about the theory of positive steps.

The third group consisted of the Scandinavian countries —Denmark, Norway, and Sweden. Being under the shadow of the German Baltic fleet, they were more or less pro-German and dared not offend Germany's ally, Japan. They feared that if the Conference adopted some common measures, they might become involved. That was why they abstained from voting on the Declaration of November 15, which provided that the States represented at Brussels must consider what was to be their common attitude in a situation where one party to an international treaty maintained its position against the views of all other parties.

The only power openly pro-Japanese was Italy. At every meeting the Italian delegate, Aldrovandi Marcscotti, tried to obstruct the work of the Conference. In his first speech, he advocated direct negotiations between China and Japan. After Japan's refusal of the second invitation to the Conference, he stated that the conference had nothing further to do. He voted against the conference declaration of November 15, as well as its report of November 24.

The remaining powers were weak and, with fewer interests in the Far East, followed the lead of the great powers. However, they professed devotion to the sanctity of treaties and supported China's just cause. Their spokesmen included Foreign Minister Spaak of Belgium and former Foreign Minister de Graeff of the Netherlands.

China did not object to mediation. The difference between China and the other powers in this respect was that after the failure of mediation, China would like the other powers to increase their aid to China and to impose some economic restrictions on Japan, such as withholding from Japan both war materiel and war credits. For that purpose, the Chinese Delegation circulated on November 13 a memorandum pointing out the vulnerability of Japan's financial and economic situation and the possible effect of economic restrictions.

The Abortive Organization of a Sub-committee

The work of the first week of the conference consisted entirely of procedural matters. The organization of a subcommittee was first discussed.

In her reply to the invitation of the Belgian government to attend the conference, Japan had emphasized that "the conference is to be attended by powers which are not directly interested in East Asia, thereby complicating the situation still further." Some delegates therefore thought that Japan might agree to participate in a small committee. Eden expressed this opinion in his opening speech, hoping that the conference would "resolve itself into a working committee and so get to grips with its task."

On November 4, at the third meeting of the conference, the Belgian minister of foreign affairs advanced the idea of organizing a subcommittee; this motion was seconded by the United States, the United Kingdom, France, and other participating countries. However, difficulties arose when the composition of the committee was discussed. The United States delegate believed that the committee should be composed only of the United States, the United Kingdom, and

Belgium, hoping that without the participation of France, Italy would be excluded. But at the insistence of France she was admitted; subsequently Italy did not want to be left out. The principal obstacle, however, was the question of the Soviet Union. The United States delegate felt that if the Soviet Union were a member of the committee, Japan would refuse to attend, but the Soviet Union was very sensitive and circulated the rumor that it might withdraw from the conference. On November 9, the United States delegate withdrew his opposition to the Soviet Union, but Litvinov, feeling that his country was discriminated against, left Brussels on the same day.

Finally it was agreed that the composition of the committee would not be decided until Japan had replied to the proposed second invitation.

The Second Invitation and Refusal

The aim of the conference was mediation. Since mediation required the presence of both parties, the conference decided to send a second invitation to Japan, this time in the name of the conference. The communication, sent on November 7, took note of the declaration of the Japanese government—that Japan harbored no territorial ambitions on China, wished to assist in the cultural and economic development of China, and intended to respect the rights of third powers in China. Nevertheless, it stated that there was a difference of opinion between China and Japan on the subject of the violation of the Nine Power Treaty. Article 7 of that treaty envisaged just such a situation, and the conference was being held for that purpose. Since the Japanese government objected that "a gathering of so many powers whose interests in East Asia are of varying degrees will only serve to complicate the situation," the conference enquired whether the Japanese government would be disposed to depute one or more representatives to exchange views with representatives of a small number of powers to be chosen for that purpose. Such exchange of views would take place

8

within the framework of the Nine Power Treaty and in conformity with the terms of the treaty.

The text of the communication was deliberately neutral. To avoid offending Japan, the text not only refrained from mentioning the League of Nations and its resolution, but even ignored Japan's military actions in China and her violation of the Nine Power Treaty. The delegate of Norway went so far as to suggest the omission of any specific mention of Article 7. Italy proposed that the conference should address communications to both parties, urging direct negotiations, with the implication that the Japanese aggression in China was no concern of the other powers. This point of view was refuted at once by the United States delegate. Nevertheless, the communication showed extraordinary forbearance, and the conference hoped against hope for Japanese participation.

Notwithstanding all the humiliations that the Conference inflicted on itself, Japan refused again to confer even with a small number of powers. In her reply of November 12, she stated that the opinion of participating powers was insufficient to persuade her to modify the views expressed in the note of October 27, namely, that her action in China was a measure of self-defense and did not come within the scope of the Nine Power Treaty. Japan could not agree to take part in a meeting based on the provisions of the treaty while she was accused of having violated the terms of that treaty.

Adoption of the First Declaration

Upon the persistent refusal of Japan to attend the conference, the participating powers felt somewhat slighted. The reaction of the conference was to study some action to counterbalance the newly announced adhesion by Italy to the Anti-Comintern Pact. Before receiving the Japanese reply, the delegates of the principal powers were already discussing (November 10-13), outside the conference, the next steps to take. On November 13, at the seventh meeting, discussing the second Japanese refusal, Koo said:

The refusal of the Japanese Government is more resolute and absolute than ever, and both the language and tone of its reply seem to indicate clearly that all the painstaking efforts of the Conference to secure her collaboration have been taken as a sign of weakness and served apparently only to inspire insolence. The claim that Japan's present action in China is resorted to as a measure of self-defense is not only a deliberate distortion of the meaning of the time-honored term, it could in no way justify her claim that the matter lay outside the scope of the Nine Power Treaty. The "full and frank communication" envisaged in Article 7 of the Treaty is intended for just such a situation. Now that the door of conciliation and mediation has been slammed in your face by the latest reply of the Japanese government, will you not decide to withhold supplies of war materiels and credit to Japan and extend aid to China? It would be a modest way in which you can fulfill your obligation of helping to check Japanese aggression and upholding the treaty in question.

Mr. Delbos stated that the Japanese reply added another problem which the conference would be compelled to consider, namely, that of one party insisting, above the voices of the other signatories of the treaty, that the treaty was not applicable in a given situation, and refusing to abide by Article 7 thereof. He added that no solution by force could, either in law or in fact, provide a lasting adjustment of relations between the two countries. Peace in the Far East, as elsewhere, was inseparable from respect for international law.

Mr. Eden said that it would be impossible for the conference to assent to the doctrine that the settlement of the conflict in the Far East was a matter for China and Japan alone. He also stated that the international situation created by Japan's reply would require careful consideration by the conference.

Mr. Davis stated that the question before the conference

was whether international relations were to be determined by arbitrary force or by law and respect for international treaties. But he still hoped Japan might see her way clear to participate in the work of the conference.

From the speeches of the three major powers at the conference, it seemed something might still be done to comply with Chinese wishes as expressed by Koo.

A long declaration was drafted by the United States delegation and submitted to the participants for transmission to their respective governments for approval. The Italian delegate argued, in vain, that another appeal should be sent to the Japanese government. Finally he voted against the declaration.

The declaration stated that the conference could not accept the view that the conflict concerned only the two countries directly involved; it was a concern in law to all parties to the Nine Power Treaty and the Pact of Paris. There existed no warrant in law for the use of armed force by any country for the purpose of intervening in the internal regime of another country, and recognition of any such a right would become a permanent cause of conflict. China was engaged in full and frank discussion with other parties of the Nine Power Treaty while Japan has refused to discuss the matter with any of them. In conclusion, the powers of the conference, having expressed their hope that Japan would not persist in her refusal, stated that they "must consider what is to be their common attitude in a situation where one party to an international treaty maintains against the views of all the other parties that the action which it has taken does not come within the scope of the treaty and sets aside provisions of the treaty which the other parties hold to be operative in the circumstances."

The words "common attitude" in the declaration provoked much apprehension among the Scandinavian countries. On November 15, the declaration was adopted by the conference with a vote of fifteen to one (Italy). The Scandinavian delegates abstained, declaring that their governments adhered to the principles of the declaration, but since they did not possess the same political interests in the Far East as certain other powers, they found it proper to abstain from voting.

The Italian opposition was a foreseen gesture, but the Scandinavian abstention demonstrated clearly to the world that the Western camp was in a complete split and that further collective action was greatly jeopardized.

The Adoption of a Report and the Final Declaration

After adopting the first declaration, the conference adjourned for a week in order that the delegates might consult their governments regarding the future activities of the conference. Mr. Eden and Mr. Delbos left Brussels, to return no more.

In the meantime, the Chinese delegation circulated a statement, based on the memorandum of November 13, reaffirming Japan's dependence on foreign supplies of war materiel and on her export and shipping trade, as well as citing her other economic and financial problems. It suggested several means by which to restrain Japan through international action—an embargo on war and industrial materials, a boycott of Japanese exports and shipping, refusal to extend credit to Japan, and the extension of economic and material aid to China—to compel Japan to abandon her policy of aggression and conquest.

This statement was circulated in the hope that the measures suggested in its contents might become the logical sequence of "common attitude" adopted in the first declaration. However, when the Conference resumed on November 22nd, it had before it a draft declaration submitted by the American, British, and French delegations. The first part of the declaration contained a summary of the previous work of the conference, but as to the second part of the declaration, Koo remarked that:

It contained nothing more than a reaffirmation of cer-

12

tain general principles. No indication was given of the common attitude which the representatives of the Conference had agreed to consider in accordance with the declaration adopted on November 15, and it contained no provision for the concrete methods of assisting China which the Chinese delegation had proposed on November 13. The Chinese delegation appeals to the conference for concrete action. Just as domestic order requires more than laws on the statute books, mere words are insufficient to restore peace and order in the face of international violence which had prompted the convocation of the present conference. It may be asked whether by its refusal to grant aid to China the Conference wishes China to cease to resist aggression or whether she should continue in her resistance without adequate means. The Chinese delegation believes that solidarity in purpose should be followed by solidarity in action, and that by such abortive ending as evidenced by the terms of the draft resolution the Conference would unwittingly augment the prevailing sense of general insecurity, rather than contribute to world order and stability.

Koo asked for time to consult his government, so the conference adjourned again on November 24. At its final session, the conference adjourned *sine die* after having adopted a report and a second declaration. Only the Italian delegation voted against it.

The report contained only a summary of the activities of the conference. The operative part of the second declaration is quoted below:

The Conference is convinced that force by itself can provide no just and lasting solution for disputes between nations. It further believes that a satisfactory settlement cannot be achieved by direct negotiations between the parties of conflict alone, and that only by consultation with other powers principally concerned can there be achieved

13

an agreement the terms of which will be just, generally acceptable and likely to endure.

The Conference strongly reaffirms the principles of the Nine Power Treaty as being among the basic principles which are essential to world peace and orderly, progressive development of national and international life.

The Conference strongly urges that hostilities be suspended and resort be made to peaceful processes.

The Conference believes that no possible step to bring about by peaceful processes a just settlement of the conflict should be overlooked or omitted.

In order to allow time for participating governments to exchange views and further explore all peaceful methods by which a just setlement of the dispute may be attained consistently with the principles of the Nine Power Treaty and in conformity with the objectives of the Treaty, the Conference deems it advisable temporarily to suspend its sittings. The conflict in the Far East remains, however, a matter of concern to all the powers assembled at Brussels and especially to those immediately and directly affected by conditions and events in the Far East.

The Conference will be called together again whenever its Chairman or any two of its members shall have reported that they consider that its deliberations can be advantageously resumed.

Under the guise of temporary adjournment, the conference was, in fact, definitely closed. With the occurrence of the subsequent events, no one could see how its deliberations could be advantageously resumed.

The disappointment of China was great, but she could not afford to vote against the declaration or to abstain; so the government instruction was to accept the declaration in the spirit of solidarity with a statement to clarify her position. Therefore, at the closing meeting of the conference, Koo made the following statement:

14

The Chinese Delegation notes that the revised text of the draft declaration contains a number of modifications and clarifications of the original text. In view of the continued raging of the hostilities in the Far East, the Chinese Delegation believes that a mere reaffirmation of the principles cannot be considered as a satisfactory result of the Conference, because it is not adequate to deal effectively with the grave situation. The Chinese Delegation regrets that the suggestions which it made to the Conference, with a view to the adoption of certain positive and concrete measures have not been considered by the Conference. The Chinese Delegation holds that such common action is indispensable in any effort to restrain the Japanese aggression and hasten the restoration of peace in the Far East. The Chinese Delegation notes that the suspension of the sittings of the Conference is only temporary and deemed advisable in order to allow time for participant Governments to exchange views and further explore all peaceful methods by which a just settlement may be attained. It is convinced that such effort should be made actively and promptly and it is indispensable to consider at the same time the necessity of common action against the aggressor. While prepared to accept the declaration in the spirit of solidarity, the Chinese Delegation requests the Conference to take note of this statement and attach it to the declaration of the Conference.

The General Atmosphere of the Conference and the Chinese Attitude

The atmosphere of the Conference may be divided into three periods. During the first period (November 3-7), ranging from the opening of the Conference to the sending of the communication to the Japanese government, the atmosphere of the conference was filled with hope of mediation and no other action was envisaged.

The second period (November 8-15) ranged from the

second Japanese refusal to the adoption of the first declaration. The reaction of the conference was rather strong after Japan's second refusal. Furthermore, the announcement of the tripartite Anti-Comintern Pact tended to reinforce the solidarity of the three Western democratic countries, namely, the United States, Great Britain, and France. The sanctity of treaty was proclaimed; a common attitude was discussed. It was hoped that some concrete attitude might be adopted to counter-balance the effect of the publication of the tripartite Anti-Comintern Pact.

The last period (November 16-24) was one of despair. During that period, the optimistic atmosphere completely disappeared. Criticism in the United States Congress made further action impossible. The departure of the British and French foreign ministers and the abstention of the three Scandinavian powers contributed to the negative attitude of the Conference, and nothing could be done but to adjourn the conference *sine die.*

Notwithstanding the changing atmosphere of the conference, the Chinese Delegation maintained its views on four points throughout:

1. *Refusal of direct negotiations.* From the beginning, Koo had insisted on the futility of direct negotiations. He further amplified the reasons on November 13:

For four years the Chinese government patiently tried to reach a peaceful settlement with Japan of the questions outstanding between them, and the present conflict is the result. For every act of concession, every gesture of conciliation on the part of China was taken by Japan as a sign of fear and led to more bullying and brow-beating. The acceptance of one demand by China was always followed by the presentation of other demands. The perpetual "dual diplomacy" practiced by Japan through the Japanese Foreign Office and the Japanese Army in her dealing with China has convinced China of the danger and futility of direct negotiations.

2. *Acceptance of legitimate mediation.* At the opening meeting of the Conference, Koo said:

China, whose love for peace is traditional, appreciates the gesture of good will of several delegations. The Chinese Government, which steadily pursued a policy of peace in the past years in the face of the most flagrant armed aggression from Japan, and which clung to that policy even in the trying days just preceding the opening of hostilities by Japan on her, has been fighting only to resist the Japanese invasion. We desire peace, but only a peace based upon the principles of the Nine Power Treaty of Washington.

Koo stated again on November 13 that "we assured the Conference from the outset of the determination of the Chinese Government to contribute its full cooperation for the restoration of peace consonant with justice." This conciliatory attitude of the Chinese Delegation had won the general sympathy and approval of the Conference.

3. *China's determination to continue the resistance.* In order to obtain a just mediation or an extension of aid to China, it was necessary to maintain China's resistance. Some delegations thought that Chinese resistance would collapse once Nanking fell. Koo reassured them on November 13:

So long as Japanese aggression persists, so long will China continue to resist. The Government and the people of China are determined to fight the aggression to the end.

4. *Extension of aid to China and imposition of some financial and economic restrictions on Japan in case of failure of mediation.* With regard to this point, Koo said in his speech of November 13:

In our struggle against the force of Japanese aggression with a whole nation behind us, resolute in purpose and undaunted in spirit, we do not ask the other signatory powers to fight for us, but we need material help to en-

17

able us to continue our effective resistance. In order to shorten the duration of hostilities and hasten the restoration of peace, it is necessary to refrain from contributing to the financial and economic resources of the aggressor and feeding him with an uninterrupted flow of arms and raw materials for his war industries.

The Causes of the Failure of the Conference

The Conference was undeniably a failure. Different causes might be traced:

1. *The divergent attitudes of the participants.* This was the principal cause of the failure of the conference. With Italy's obstruction, the Scandinavian countries' aloofness, and the Soviet Union's passive attitude after her proposed exclusion from the subcommittee—all indicated that it was not possible to adopt common concrete measures.

2. *The lack of leadership.* In the 30's, Great Britain was still the leading power in the Far East, but because the European situation was already grave, she hoped that the United States might take the lead in the Far East. Since the United States was the sponsor of the Nine Power Treaty and President Roosevelt had just made his famous "quarantine" speech at Chicago (October 5, 1937), Britain thought this was not too much to ask. But owing to the attitude of the Congress, the United States was reluctant to take the position of leader. Thus the conference had no directing power.

3. *The negative attitude of the United States Congress.* Being a prosperous country, the United States did not wish to be involved in a war. On November 15, when the Congress opened its session, the isolationists were very active, threatening the application of the Neutrality Act and proposing to amend the Constitution by giving the power of declaring war to the direct vote of the people. Thus the policy of the United States government for international co-operation received a severe blow. Mr. Davis, the United States delegate, was personally attacked by some members

of the Congress; he felt very depressed and dared not suggest any positive action.

4. *The deterioration of the Chinese military situation.* On November 19, the Chinese army evacuated Shanghai after putting up a magnificent but costly resistance against the far superior forces of the aggressor. On November 20, with the Japanese advancing toward Nanking, the transfer of the capital to Chungking was announced. The psychological effect on the minds of the various delegations was great. They thought that China was on the eve of collapse and that after the eventual fall of Nanking (which actually fell on December 13 of the same year), the Chinese resistance might be broken. Although the Chinese Delegation tried hard to reassure them that her resistance would continue, they were somewhat skeptical. In these circumstances, everyone hesitated to be involved in an apparently losing war. It may be recalled that at the beginning of the conference, the Chinese Delegation, seeing that the evacuation of Shanghai planned by the Chinese government would adversely affect the morale of the Conference, cabled to the government to hold the position as long as possible in order not to give a pretext for inaction to the different delegations. During the prolonged period of holding the military position, China's losses were very heavy. However, China continued her resistance until the eventual Allied victory, as predicted by her Delegation at that time.

Some Results of the Conference

After the Lukouchiao incident, which signalled the beginning of large-scale attacks on China by the Japanese armed forces, the Conference was the first important international gathering specially convened for solving the Sino-Japanese dispute. The Chinese government and people put great hope on the Conference. On the other hand, in view of the divergent attitudes of the different delegations, the task of the Chinese Delegation was unusually difficult.

19

Nevertheless the Conference served a useful purpose in some respects. To confirm this view we may quote the statement made by Norman Davis in his report to the Secretary of State of the United States on December 16, 1937, and published by the United States government in the pamphlet "The Conference at Brussels":

The outstanding achievements of the Conference were as follows:

1. Exchange of views among nineteen governments, enabling the delegate of each, and through them their governments, to obtain knowledge of the attitude and position of the others;

2. Demonstration of the unwillingness of Japan to resort to methods of conciliation;

3. Clarification of the fact that the Japanese continue to insist that the issues between Japan and China are exclusive to those two countries whereas the Conference powers, with the exception of Italy, deny this and affirm that the situation is of concern to all of them and in fact to all members of the family of nations;

4. Express reaffirmation by the Conference Powers, with the exception of Italy, of the principles of the Nine Power Treaty;

5. Express serving of notice that the settlement ultimately arrived at must be consistent with the principles of the Nine Power Treaty and satisfactory to the Conference Powers;

6. Express serving of notice that the Conference Powers will continue to concern themselves with the situation and that the Conference is not ended but is in recess and is subject to reconvocation.

Appendix I

THE NINE POWER TREATY of WASHINGTON, 1922

The United States of America, Belgium, The British Empire, China, France, Italy, Japan, The Netherlands and Portugal:

Desiring to adopt a policy designed to stabilise conditions in the Far East, to safeguard the rights and interests of China, and to promote intercourse between China and the other Powers upon the basis of equality of opportunity:

Have resolved to conclude a treaty for that purpose . . .

Article I.

The Contracting Powers, other than China, agree:

(1) To respect the sovereignty, the independence, and the territorial and administrative integrity of China;

(2) To provide the fullest and most unembarrassed opportunity to China to develop and maintain for herself an effective and stable government;

(3) To use their influence for the purpose of effectually establishing and maintaining the principle of equal opportunity for the commerce and industry of all nations throughout the territory of China;

(4) To refrain from taking advantage of conditions in China in order to seek special rights or privileges which would abridge the rights of subjects or citizens of friendly States, and from countenancing action inimical to the security of such States.

Article II.

The Contracting Powers agree not to enter into any treaty, agreement, arrangement or understanding, either with one another, or, individually or collectively, with any Power or Powers, which would infringe or impair the principles stated in Article I.

Article III.

With a view to applying more effectually the principles of the Open Door or equality of opportunity in China for the trade and industry of all nations, the Contracting Powers, other than China, agree that they will not seek, nor support their respective nationals in seeking—

a) any arrangement which might purport to establish in favour of their interests any general superiority of rights with respect to commercial or economic development in any designated region of China;

b) any such monopoly or preference as would deprive the nationals of any other Power of the right of undertaking any legitimate trade or industry in China, or of participating with the Chinese Government, or with any authority, in any category of public enterprise, or which by reason of its scope, duration or geographical extent is calculated to frustrate the practical application of the principle of equal opportunity.

It is understood that the foregoing stipulations of this Article are not to be so construed as to prohibit the acquisition of such properties or rights as may be necessary to the conduct of a particular commercial, industrial or financial undertaking or to the encouragement of invention and research.

China undertakes to be guided by the principles stated in the foregoing stipulations of this Article in dealing with applications for economic rights and privileges from Governments and nationals of all foreign countries, whether parties to the present Treaty or not.

Article IV.

The Contracting Powers agree not to support any agreements by their respective nationals with each other designed to create Spheres of Influence or to provide for the enjoyment of mutually exclusive opportunities in designated parts of Chinese territory.

Article V.

China agrees that, throughout the whole of the railways in China, she will not exercise or permit unfair discrimination of any kind. In particular there shall be no discrimination whatever, direct or indirect, in respect of charges or of facilities on the ground of the nationality of passengers or the countries from which or to which they are proceeding, or the origin or ownership of goods or the country from which or to which they are consigned, or the nationality or ownership of the ship or other means of conveying such passengers or goods before or after their transport on the Chinese Railways.

The Contracting Powers, other than China, assume a corresponding obligation in respect of any of the aforesaid railways over which they or their nationals are in a position to exercise any control in virtue of any concession, special agreement or otherwise.

Article VI.

The Contracting Powers, other than China, agree fully to respect China's rights as a neutral in time of war to which China will observe the obligations of neutrality.

Article VII.

The Contracting Powers agree that, whenever a situation arises which in the opinion of any one of them involves the application of the stipulations of the present Treaty, and renders desirable discussion of such application, there shall be full and frank communication between the Contracting Powers concerned.

Article VIII.

Powers not signatory to the present Treaty, which have Governments recognized by the Signatory Powers and which have treaty relations with China, shall be invited to adhere to the present Treaty. To this end the Government of the United States will make the necessary communications to the non-signatory Powers and will inform the Contracting Powers of the replies received. Adherence by any Power shall become effective on receipt of notice thereof by the Government of the United States.

Article IX.

The present Treaty shall be rectified by the Contracting Powers in accordance with their respective constitutional methods and shall take effect on the date of the deposit of all the ratifications which shall take place at Washington as soon as possible. The Government of the United States will transmit to the other Contracting Powers a certified copy of the procès-verbal of the deposit of ratifications.

The present Treaty of which the French and English texts are both authentic, shall remain deposited in the archives of the Government of the United States, and duly certified copies thereof shall be transmitted by that Government to the other Contracting Powers.

In faith whereof the above-named Plenipotentiaries have signed the present Treaty.

Done at the City of Washington the Sixth day of February, One Thousand Nine Hundred and Twenty-Two.

Appendix II

Report of the Conference
November 24, 1937

1. The Conference at Brussels was assembled pursuant to an invitation extended by the Belgian Government at the request of His Majesty's Government in the United Kingdom with the approval of the American Government. It held its opening session on November 3, 1937. The Conference has now reached a point at which it appears desirable to record the essential phases of its work.

2. In the winter of 1921-22 there were signed at Washington a group of inter-related treaties and agreements of which the Nine Power Treaty regarding principles and policies to be followed in matters concerning China constituted one of the most important units. These treaties and agreements were the result of careful deliberation and were entered upon freely. They were designed primarily to bring about conditions of stability and security in the Pacific area.

The Nine Power Treaty stipulated in Article I that "the Contracting Powers, other than China, agree:

(1) To respect the sovereignty, the independence, and the territorial and administrative integrity of China;

(2) To provide the fullest and most unembarrassed opportunity to China to develop and maintain for herself an effective and stable government;

(3) To use their influence for the purpose of effectually establishing and maintaining the principle of equal opportunity for the commerce and industry of all nations throughout the territory of China;

(4) To refrain from taking advantage of conditions in China in order to seek special rights or privileges which would abridge the rights of subjects or citizens of friendly States, and from countenancing action inimical to the security of such States."

Under and in the light of these undertakings and of the provisions contained in the other treaties, the situation in the Pacific area was for a decade characterized by a substantial measure of stability, with considerable progress toward the other objectives envisaged in the treaties. In recent years there have come a series of conflicts between Japan and China, and these conflicts have culminated in the hostilities now in progress.

3. The Conference at Brussels was called for the purpose, as set forth in the terms of the invitation "of examining in accordance with Article VII of the Nine Power Treaty, the situation in the Far East and to consider friendly peaceable methods for hastening the end of the regrettable conflict now taking place there." With the exception of Japan, all of the signatories and adherents to the Nine Power Treaty of February 6, 1922, accepted the invitation and sent representatives to Brussels, for the purpose stated in the invitation.

4. The Chinese Government, attending the Conference and participating in its deliberations, has communicated with the other parties to the Nine Power Treaty in conformity with Article VII of that Treaty. It has stated here that its present military operations are purely in resistance to armed invasion of China by Japan. It has declared its willingness to accept a peace based upon the principles of the Nine Power Treaty and to collaborate wholeheartedly with the other Powers in support of the principle of the sanctity of treaties.

5. The Japanese Government, in replying with regret that it was not able to accept the invitation to the Conference, affirmed that "the action of Japan in China is a measure of self-defense which she has been compelled to

take in the face of China's fierce anti-Japanese policy and practice, and especially by her provocative action in resorting to force of arms; and consequently it lies, as has been declared already by the Imperial Government, outside the purview of the Nine Power Treaty"; and advanced the view that an attempt to seek a solution at a gathering of so many Powers "would only serve to complicate the situation still further and to put serious obstacles in the path of a just and proper solution."

6. On November 7, 1937, the Conference sent, through the Belgian Government, to the Japanese Government, a communication in the course of which the Conference inquired whether the Japanese Government would be willing to depute a representative or representatives to exchange views with representatives of a small number of Powers to be chosen for that purpose, the exchange of views to take place within the framework of the Nine Power Treaty and in conformity with the provisions of that treaty, toward throwing further light on points of difference and facilitating a settlement of the Sino-Japanese conflict. In that communication the representatives of the States met at Brussels expressed their earnest desire that peaceful settlement be achieved.

7. To that communication the Japanese Government replied in a communication of November 12, 1937, stating that it could not do otherwise than maintain its previously expressed point of view that the present action of Japan in her relations with China was a measure of self-defense and did not come within the scope of the Nine Power Treaty; that only an effort between the two parties would constitute a means of securing the most just and the most equitable settlement, and that the intervention of a collective organ such as the Conference would merely excite public opinion in the two countries and make it more difficult to reach a solution satisfactory to all.

8. On November 15, the Conference adopted a declaration in the course of which it affirmed that the representa-

tives of the Union of South Africa, the United States of America, Australia, Belgium, Bolivia, Canada, China, France, the United Kingdom, India, Mexico, Netherlands, New Zealand, Portugal and the Union of Socialist Soviet Republics ". . . consider that this conflict of concern in law to all countries party to the Nine Power Treaty of Washington of 1922 and to all countries party to the Pact of Paris of 1928 and of concern in fact to all countries members of the family of nations."

9. In the presence of this difference between the views of the Conference and of the Japanese Government there now appears to be no opportunity at this time for the Conference to carry out its terms of reference insofar as they relate to entering into discussions with Japan towards bringing about peace by agreement. The Conference therefore is concluding this phase of its work and at this moment of going into recess adopts a further declaration of its views.

10. The text of the communication sent to the Japanese Government on November 7th, 1937, reads as follows:

(1) The representatives of the States met in Brussels on November 3rd last have taken cognisance of the reply which the Japanese Government sent in on October 27th to the invitation of the Belgian Government, and the statement which accompanied this reply.

(2) In these documents the Imperial Government states that it cherishes no territorial ambitions in respect of China and that on the contrary it sincerely desires "to assist in the material and moral development of the Chinese nation," that it also desires "to promote cultural and economic co-operation" with the foreign Powers in China and that it intends furthermore scrupulously "to respect foreign rights and interests in that country."

(3) The points referred to in this declaration are among the fundamental principles of the Treaty of Washington of February 6, 1922 (the Nine Power Treaty). The representatives of the States parties to this Treaty have

taken note of the declarations of the Imperial Government in this respect.

(4) The Imperial Government moreover denies that there can be any question of a violation of the Nine Power Treaty by Japan and it formulates a number of complaints against the Chinese Government. The Chinese Government for its part contends that there has been violation, denies the charges of the Japanese Government and, in turn, makes complaint against Japan.

(5) The Treaty has made provision for just such a situation. It should be borne in mind that the exchange of views taking place in Brussels is based essentially on these provisions and constitutes "full and frank communication" as envisaged in Article VII. This Conference is being held with a view to assisting in the resolving by peaceful means of a conflict between parties to the Treaty.

One of the parties to the present conflict, China, is represented at the Conference and has affirmed its willingness fully to co-operate in its work.

The Conference regrets the absence of the other party, Japan, whose co-operation is most desirable.

(6) The Imperial Government states that it is "firmly convinced that an attempt to seek a solution at a gathering of so many Powers whose interests in East Asia are of varying degree, or who have practically no interests there at all, will only serve to complicate the situation still further and to put serious obstacles in the path of a just and proper solution."

It should be pointed out that all of these Powers which are parties to the Treaty are, under the terms of this instrument, entitled to exercise the rights which the Treaty confers upon them; that all Powers which have interests in the Far East are concerned regarding the present hostilities; and that the whole world is solicitous with regard to the effect of these hostilities on the peace and security of the members of the nations.

However, the representatives of the States met at

Brussels believe that it may be possible to allay Japan's misgivings referred to above; they would be glad to know whether the Imperial Government would be disposed to depute a representative or representatives to exchange views with representatives of a small number of Powers to be chosen for that purpose. Such an exchange of views would take place within the framework of the Nine Power Treaty and in conformity with the provisions of that Treaty. Its aims would be to throw further light on the various points referred to above and to facilitate a settlement of the conflict. Regretting the continuation of hostilities, being firmly convinced that a peaceful settlement is alone capable of ensuring a lasting and constructive solution of the present conflict, and having confidence in the efficacy of methods of conciliation, the representatives of the States met at Brussels earnestly desire that such a settlement may be achieved.

(7) The States represented at the Conference would be very glad to know as soon as possible the attitude of the Imperial Government towards this proposal.

11. The text of the declaration adopted by the Conference on November 15, 1937, reads as follows:

The Representatives of the Union of South Africa, the United States of America, Australia, Belgium, Bolivia, Canada, China, France, The United Kingdom, India, Mexico, Netherlands, New Zealand, Portugal and the Union of Socialist Soviet Republics have drawn up the following declaration:

(1) The representatives of the above-mentioned States met at Brussels, having taken cognisance of the Japanese Government's reply of November 12, 1937, to the communication addressed to the latter on November 7, 1937, observe with regret that the Japanese Government still contends that the conflict between Japan and China lies outside the scope of the Nine Power Treaty and again declines to enter into an exchange of views for the purpose of endeavoring to achieve a peaceful settlement of that conflict.

(2) It is clear that the Japanese concept of the issues and interests involved in the conflict under reference is utterly different from the concept of most of the other nations and governments of the world. The Japanese Government insist that, as the conflict is between Japan and China, it concerns those two countries only. Against this, the representatives of the above-mentioned States now met at Brussels consider this conflict of concern in law to all countries party to the Nine Power Treaty of Washington of 1922 and to all countries party to the Pact of Paris of 1928, and of concern in fact to all countries members of the family of Nations.

(3) It cannot be denied that in the Nine Power Treaty the parties thereto affirmed it to be their desire to adopt a specified policy designed to stabilize conditions in the Far East and agreed to apply certain specified principles in their relations with China and, in China, with one another; and that in the Pact of Paris the parties agreed that "the settlement or solution of all disputes or conflicts of whatever nature or of whatever origin they may be, which may arise among them, shall never be sought except by pacific means."

(4) It cannot be denied that the present hostilities between Japan and China adversely affect not only the rights of all nations but also the material interests of nearly all nations. These hostilities have brought to some nationals of third countries death, to many nationals of third countries great peril, to property of nationals of third countries widespread destruction, to international communications disruption, to international trade disturbance and loss, to the peoples of all nations a sense of horror and indignation, to all the world feelings of uncertainty and apprehension.

(5) The representatives of the above-mentioned States met at Brussels therefore regard these hostilities and the situation which they have brought about as matters inevitably of concern to the countries which they represent

and—more—to the whole world. To them the problem appears not in terms simply of relations between two countries in the Far East but in terms of law, orderly processes, world security and world peace.

(6) The Japanese Government has affirmed in its note of October 27th, to which it refers in its note of November 12th, that in employing armed force against China it was anxious to "make China renounce her present policy." The representatives of the above-mentioned States met at Brussels are moved to point out that there exists no warrant in law for the use of armed force by any country for the purpose of intervening in the internal regime of another country and that general recognition of such a right would be a permanent cause of conflict.

(7) The Japanese Government contends that it should be left to Japan and China to proceed to a settlement by and between themselves alone. But, that a just and lasting settlement could be achieved by such a method cannot be believed. Japanese armed forces are present in enormous numbers on Chinese soil and have occupied large and important areas thereof. Japanese authorities have declared in substance that it is Japan's objective to destroy the will and the ability of China to resist the will and demands of Japan. The Japanese Government affirms that it is China whose actions and attitude are in contravention of the Nine Power Treaty; yet, whereas China is engaged in full and frank discussion of the matter with the other parties to that Treaty, Japan refuses to discuss it with any of them. Chinese authorities have repeatedly declared that they will not, in fact that they cannot, negotiate with Japan alone for a settlement by agreement. In these circumstances, there is no ground for any belief that, if left to themselves, Japan and China would arrive in the appreciably near future at any solution which would give promise of peace between those two countries, security for the rights and interests of other countries, and political and economic stability in the Far East. On the contrary, there

is every reason to believe that if this matter were left entirely to Japan and China the armed conflict—with attendant destruction of life and property, disorder, uncertainty, instability, suffering, enmity, hatred and disturbance to the whole world—would continue indefinitely.

(8) The Japanese Government, in their latest communication, invite the Powers represented at Brussels to make a contribution to the stability of Eastern Asia in accordance with the realities of the situation.

(9) In the view of the representatives of the above-mentioned States met at Brussels, the essential realities of the situation are those to which they draw attention above.

(10) The representatives of the above-mentioned States met at Brussels are firmly of the belief that, for the reasons given above, a just and durable settlement is not to be expected of direct negotiations between the parties. That is why, in the communications addressed to the Japanese Government, they invited that Government to confer with them or with representatives of a small number of Powers to be chosen for that purpose, in the hope that such exchange of views might lead to acceptance of their good offices and thus help towards the negotiation of a satisfactory settlement.

(11) They will believe that if the parties to the conflict would agree to a cessation of hostilities in order to give an opportunity for such a procedure to be tried, success might be achieved. The Chinese Delegation has intimated its readiness to fall in with this procedure. The representatives of the States met at Brussels find it difficult to understand Japan's persistent refusal to discuss such a method.

(12) Though hoping that Japan will not adhere to her refusal the above-mentioned States represented at Brussels must consider what is to be their common attitude in a situation where one party to an international treaty maintains against the views of all the other parties that the action which it has taken does not come within the scope

of that treaty and sets aside provisions of the treaty which the other parties hold to be operative in the circumstances.

The representatives of Sweden made the following statement:

"No one can regret more deeply than does the Swedish Government the fact that the Conference's efforts at mediation have so far remained without result. Having to take note of this fact, my Government, which adheres to the principles of the declaration but which does not possess the same political interests in the Far East as certain other Powers, feels that it is its duty to abstain from voting for this text."

The representative of Norway made the following statement:

"The Norwegian Government accepted the invitation to this Conference in the desire thereby to contribute if possible to a settlement of the conflict in the Far East by peaceful mediation.

"Nobody deplores more than my Government that the efforts of the Conference towards such mediation have hitherto been fruitless.

"I am quite in accord with the principles underlying the declaration before us and the venture to express the hope that it may still prove possible to obtain through mediation a settlement on the basis of those principles.

"Referring, however, to my previous declaration made on the 13th instant, I find it proper to abstain from voting."

The representative of Denmark made the following statement:

"I should like to associate myself with the statements just made by my colleagues from Sweden and Norway. Also my country deplores that the efforts for mediation have hitherto not met with success, and I fully share the hope that through means of mediation it may still be possible to obtain some results. For similar reasons as those given by my Scandinavian colleagues, also I think it proper to abstain from voting on the text of this declaration, while fully in accord with the principles laid down therein."

The representative of Italy made the following statement:

"Italy considers the declaration before us as a door open not towards the settlement of the conflict, but rather towards the most serious complications.

"Italy does not intend to assume the responsibilities that might devolve therefrom, and she therefore expresses her definitely contrary vote, whilst reserving her attitude as regards all that concerns the subsequent phases of the dispute."

12. The text of the declaration adopted by the Conference on November 24, 1937, reads as follows:

(1) The Nine Power Treaty is a conspicuous example of numerous international instruments by which the nations of the world enunciate certain principles and accept certain self-denying rules in their conduct with each other solemnly undertaking to respect the sovereignty of other nations, to refrain from seeking political or economic domination of other nations, and to abstain from interference in their internal affairs.

(2) These international instruments constitute a framework within which international security and international peace are intended to be safeguarded without resort to arms and within which international friendships should subsist on the basis of mutual trust, goodwill, and beneficial trade and financial relations.

(3) It must be recognized that whenever armed force is employed in disregard of these principles the whole structure of international relations based upon the safeguards provided by treaties is disturbed. Nations are then compelled to seek security in ever-increasing armaments. There is created everywhere a feeling of uncertainty and insecurity. The validity of these principles cannot be destroyed by force, their universal applicability cannot be

denied, and their indispensability to civilization and progress cannot be gainsaid.

(4) It was in accordance with these principles that this Conference was called in Brussels for the purpose, as set forth in the terms of the invitation issued by the Belgian Government, "of examining, in accordance with Article VII of the Nine Power Treaty, the situation in the Far East and to consider friendly methods for hastening the end of the regrettable conflict now taking place there."

(5) Since its opening session on November 3rd the Conference has continuously striven to promote conciliation and has endeavoured to secure the co-operation of the Japanese Government in the hope of arresting hostilities and bringing about a settlement.

(6) The Conference is convinced that force by itself can provide no just and lasting solution for disputes between nations. It continues to believe that it would be to the immediate and the ultimate interest of both parties to the present dispute to avail themselves of the assistance of others in an effort to bring hostilities to an early end as a necessary preliminary to the achievement of a general and lasting settlement. It further believes that a satisfactory settlement cannot be achieved by direct negotiation between the parties to the conflict alone, and that only by consultation with other Powers principally concerned can there be achieved an agreement the terms of which will be just, generally acceptable and likely to endure.

(7) This Conference strongly reaffirms the principles of the Nine Power Treaty as being among the basic principles which are essential to world peace and orderly progressive development of national and international life.

(8) The Conference believes that a prompt suspension of hostilities in the Far East would be in the best interests not only of China and Japan but of all nations. With each day's continuance of the conflict the loss in lives and property increases and the ultimate solution of the conflict becomes more difficult.

(9) The Conference therefore strongly urges that hostilities be suspended and resort be had to peaceful processes.

(10) The Conference believes that no possible step to bring about by peaceful processes a just settlement of the conflict should be overlooked or omitted.

(11) In order to allow time for participating Governments to exchange views and further explore all peaceful methods by which a just settlement of the dispute may be attained consistently with the principles of the Nine Power Treaty, and in conformity with the objectives of that Treaty, the Conference deems it advisable temporarily to suspend its sittings. The conflict in the Far East remains, however, a matter of concern to all of the Powers assembled at Brussels—by virtue of commitments in the Nine Power Treaty or of special interest in the Far East—and especially to those most immediately and directly affected by conditions and events in the Far East. Those of them that are parties to the Nine Power Treaty have expressly adopted a policy designed to stabilize conditions in the Far East and, to that end, are bound by the provisions of that Treaty, outstanding among which are those of Articles I and VII.

(12) The Conference will be called together again whenever its Chairman or any two of its members shall have reported that they consider that its deliberations can be advantageously resumed.

Asia in the Modern World

Monograph Series

No. 1. THE CHINESE REVOLUTION OF 1911 by C. T. Liang — A lucid account of the most important event in China's contemporary history — $1.00.

No. 2. CHINA AT THE PARIS PEACE CONFERENCE, 1919 by Wunsz King — A study based on extensive research in source materials heretofore unpublished in Western languages — $1.00.

No. 3. CHINA AT THE WASHINGTON CONFERENCE, 1921-1922 by Wunsz King—A critical study which describes and recreates one of the major moments in Far Eastern international affairs — $1.25.

No. 4. CHINA AND THE NINE POWER CONFERENCE AT BRUSSELS in 1937 by Tsien Tai — An historical account vital for understanding the true nature of the Sino-Japanese dispute prior to World War II – $1.25.

Orders should be sent to:

St. John's University Press
Grand Central and Utopia Parkways
Jamaica, New York 11432